Ultimate Pittsburgh Trivia

1,000 answers to:
What makes Pittsburgh so interesting?

by

Dane Topich

TOWERS MAGUIRE PUBLISHING

a division of The Local History Company

Pittsburgh, Pennsylvania, USA

Ultimate Pittsburgh Trivia
Copyright © 2007 by Dane Topich

Published by
Towers Maguire Publishing
(a division of The Local History Company)
112 North Woodland Road
Pittsburgh, PA 15232
www.TowersMaguire.com   www.TheLocalHistoryCompany.com
info@TowersMaguire.com   info@TheLocalHistoryCompany.com

The names "Towers Maguire Publishing", "The Local History Company", "Publishers of History and Heritage", and its logo are trademarks of The Local History Company.

Cover photo by Tim Fabian.

   ISBN-13: 978-0-9770429-5-1
   ISBN-10: 0-9770429-5-2
Library of Congress Cataloging-in-Publication Data

Topich, Dane, 1940-
    Ultimate Pittsburgh Trivia / Dane Topich.—1st ed.
        p.   cm.
    Includes index.
    ISBN-13: 978-0-9770429-5-1 (soft cover : alk. paper) ISBN-10: 0-9770429-5-2
    (soft cover : alk. paper) 1. Pittsburgh (Pa.)—Miscellanea. 2. Pittsburgh (Pa.)—
    Pictorial works. I. Title.
F159.P645T67 2006
974.8'86—dc22

                              2006025477

Printed in USA

C O N T E N T S

ACKNOWLEDGMENTS

I'd like to thank the following for their help in assembling this book:

Dana Barnes

Bill Berner

James Burch

Darlene DiBenedetto

Sam Eisnitz

Frank "Mousey" Fennell

Tracy Konieczny

Jeff Leber

Jack Moore

Stanley Niebrzydowski

Jackie O'Connor

Jim Pulford

RealSTATs

Jeff Weissert

Stanley "Zites" Zaidel

Christine Cooper, Mandy Fields, Emily DeVore, Megan Boyd, Cheryl Towers, and Harold Maguire: the Towers Maguire Publishing crew.

A special thanks to the Carnegie Library of Pittsburgh, Pennsylvania Department.

DEDICATION

To my seven sisters, one brother, one sister-in-law, all my brothers-in-law, and my 67 nieces, nephews, great-nieces and great-nephews, and Mildred Tepovich Dojonovic, 1910-2006, a classy, dignified nonagenarian.

Dane Topich

INTRODUCTION

If Pittsburgh were situated somewhere in the heart of Europe, tourists would eagerly journey hundreds of miles out of their way to visit it.

Brendan Gill, writing in *The New Yorker*

Pittsburgh is my home town and its beauty and history have always fascinated me. During my years as editorial director and public affairs manager for KDKA-TV and radio and before that while working in political campaigns, I started to collect trivia. It began innocently enough with a few odd facts here and there that made for good conversation— "Did you know?" I'd say as a way of getting started.

I began putting these tidbits on paper as the number of items grew. Eventually I realized that I had a disease on my hands and maybe even a book, confirmed when I handed a manuscript to a buddy to read and he wouldn't give it back because he wanted to share it with friends. While he passed it around, I simply kept on collecting, finally winnowing the lot to what you hold in your hands. I hope that you enjoy reading them—and stumping your friends—as much as I enjoyed discovering them. And if you're a researcher or fact checker, this one's for you!

Dane Topich

CELEBRITIES FROM THE START

Why is Jackson smiling? Courtesy Pittsburgh Zoo and PPG Aquarium.

In what Pittsburgh neighborhood was former Miami Dolphin's quarterback Dan Marino born and from what high school did he graduate?

Marino was born in the Oakland section of Pittsburgh and is a graduate of Oakland's Central Catholic. He was a standout player at the University of Pittsburgh, also located in Oakland.

Which famous area actor at one time worked as a stagehand at WQED-TV?

Michael Keaton. Keaton was born in Coraopolis, PA and graduated from Montour High School in 1969. He did his stagehand work without a mask or cape.

Which Pittsburgh-born author was awarded the 1975 Pulitzer Prize in Nonfiction for her book *Pilgrim at Tinker Creek*?

Annie Dillard.

He was born nearby Indiana, Pennsylvania. He married Gloria. He traveled to Washington under a very common fictitious name. His work is on view regularly during the Christmas season. He is a retired Air Force general. Who is he?

Jimmy Stewart. Indiana now has a museum featuring much of his memorabilia.

How many former national heads of the National Organization for Women (NOW) have roots in the Pittsburgh area?

Three. They are Molly Yard, Ellie Smeal and Wilma Scott Heide.

What Pittsburgh area school is named after the "Financier of the American Revolution," someone who, incidentally, ended up in debtor's prison for more than three years?

Robert Morris. Evidently, not every decision he made was financially sound.

Which 1980 Carnegie Mellon University graduate won an Oscar in 1994 for her role in *The Piano*?

Holly Hunter.

Which veteran of NBC's *Saturday Night Live* "Weekend Update" attended Point Park College and made his debut on KDKA-TV in 1979?

Dennis Miller.

Mark Stutzman is a 1979 graduate of the Art Institute of Pittsburgh. For a while, he worked as a graphic artist at KDKA-TV. But he's most famous for what?

Designing the postage stamp depicting American rock and roll icon Elvis Presley.

Ralph E. Dias, Michael J. Estocin, John G. Gertsch, James A. Graham, William Morgan, Michael J. Novosel, William Port, William R. Prom, and David F. Winder all come from Western Pennsylvania and all have won the Medal of Honor for bravery in combat. In what war did they receive their medals?

Vietnam.

Who was the last person from Allegheny County to receive the U.S. Medal of Honor for military heroism?

Michael J. Novosel, who was born in Etna, received the medal for bravery in the Vietnam War. He performed his heroics in 1969. Novosel fought not only in Vietnam, but also in World War II and Korea.

How many transplants has Dr. Tom Starzl performed throughout his career?

Dr. Starzl says he stopped counting years ago and has no idea.

Who performed Pennsylvania's first successful heart transplant and when? What else was he noted for?

Dr. Henry T. Bahnson, chairman of the University of Pittsburgh Medical Center Department of Surgery. The operation took place in 1968 and the patient, Pittsburgher Ben Anolik, lived another 14 months. Bahnson was also noted for climbing Mount Everest and Mount McKinley, among others.

Sam Malone tended bar at a "cheerful" Boston bistro for a while, but before that job he was a student at Carnegie Mellon University where nearly everybody knew his name as what?

Ted Danson.

Orrin Hatch is a United States Senator from Utah. From what high school and law school did he graduate?

Baldwin High School in Allegheny County and the University of Pittsburgh's School of Law.

This ex-police officer, originally from East Pittsburgh, walked over the thin blue line and became a best selling novelist, specializing in crime thrillers. Who is he?

Joseph Wambaugh. He wrote The Thin Blue Line, Onion Field *and* Choir Boys, *among others.*

Penn Hills native Sid McGinnis plays his guitar five nights a week on the CBS television network. On what show does McGinnis appear?

Late Night with David Letterman. *He sometimes wears a Pittsburgh Pirates' hat or jersey on camera.*

Which Carnegie Mellon University professor won the Nobel Prize for Economics yet never taught economics?

Herbert Simon.

He might have achieved success as the author of *Slaughterhouse Five* and *Player Piano*, but this author was not too successful at what was then called Carnegie Tech. He flunked thermodynamics. Who is he?

Kurt Vonnegut.

How many bishops who have served as the head of Pittsburgh's Roman Catholic Diocese went on to become cardinals?

There were three: John Dearden, John Wright and Anthony Bevilacqua. Donald W. Wuerl, named archbishop of the Washington, DC diocese in May, 2006, may become the fourth. Historically, the head of the Washington diocese has become a cardinal.

Who is the only Pittsburgh area-born priest to become a cardinal in the Roman Catholic Church?

Cardinal Adam Maida, who was elevated to the post on February 26, 1994.

Dr. Stanley Pearle graduated from Pittsburgh's Schenley High School in 1936. What is he known for today?

He is the founder of Pearle Vision, the national chain of eyeglass stores based in Dallas, Texas.

How did Pittsburgh's premier hair stylist, Philip Pelusi, begin his career?

He was a sheet metal worker for four years.

In the early 1970s, when national talk show host Rush Limbaugh worked as a disc jockey at Pittsburgh area radio station WIXZ, he went by a different name. What name did he use?

Jeff Christy.

John Nash, the subject of the book and movie *A Beautiful Mind,* is a graduate of what local institution?

Nash graduated from CMU (known then as Carnegie Tech) in 1948 with a degree in mathematics.

What is the name of the Pittsburgh police officer who directed downtown traffic in the 1970s and '80s with highly distinctive hand signals and gestures as well as with body language and facial reactions? He even made an appearance on *Candid Camera* and was featured in the movie *Flashdance*.

Vic Cianca.

The NBA Dallas Mavericks are owned by a 1976 Mount Lebanon High School graduate. Before owning the Mavericks, this entrepreneur owned Broadcast.com which he sold to Yahoo! for $5.7 billion in stock in 1999. He sold another company to CompuServe. What is his name?

Mark Cuban.

The USS *Pittsburgh*, a 13,600-ton cruiser, participated in three major military operations in the Pacific in World War II. Name at least one.

1. Iwo Jima

2. Airstrikes against airfields and other military installations on the Japanese island of Kyushu.

3. Okinawa

In June 1945, the Pittsburgh *lost her bow in a typhoon. The bow, nick-named "McKeesport," was salvaged and brought to Guam, and* Pittsburgh *returned to the U.S. with a false bow. The ship was decommissioned in 1956 and scrapped in 1974.*

What is the USS *Pittsburgh* today?

It is a fast attack nuclear powered submarine carrying torpedoes and tomahawk missiles. It was commissioned on November 23, 1985.

USS Pittsburgh. *Courtesy United States Navy.*

Yuan Chang and Patrick S. Moore, a husband and wife research team at the University of Pittsburgh Cancer Institute, discovered what virus?

They discovered Kaposi's sarcoma-associated herpes virus (KSHV) which causes Kaposi's sarcoma, the most common malignancy in AIDS patients.

Between 1977 and 1982, these two scholars wrote two papers (one while both were at Carnegie Mellon University) that served as a critique of Keynesian theory, which argues that changes in demand, especially consumer demand, play the greatest role in the economic cycle. Their papers won them the Nobel Prize for Economics in 2004. Who are they?

Finn E. Kydland met Edward C. Prescott at CMU when Kydland was studying for his PhD and Prescott served as his advisor. Both earned their doctorates at CMU.

Paul C. Lauterbur, who worked at the Mellon Institute (now part of Carnegie Mellon University), received a PhD in chemistry from the University of Pittsburgh in 1962 and lived for a while in the city's Oakland section. He was awarded the 2003 Nobel Prize in Physiology or Medicine for his work in what field?

Magnetic resonance imaging (MRI). Lauterbur shared the prize with another scientist. He is now on the faculty at the University of Illinois.

Herbert Boyer graduated from high school in Derry (Westmoreland County), PA and received degrees from Saint Vincent College and the University of Pittsburgh. In the 1970s, Boyer and an associate devised a way to recombine segments of DNA. This genetic engineering technique led to the formation of the biotechnology industry and to the start of one of the U.S.'s first biotech companies. What cutting-edge company did Boyer help begin?

Genentech. The name stands for "genetic engineering technology." The company was incorporated in 1976.

Because of his prowess, to say nothing of his propensity, Jackson, a bull elephant at the Pittsburgh Zoo and Aquarium, gets to leave his home periodically to go to work. What is his job, his avocation really? (Hint: his job requires only two of his feet to be on the ground.)

Jackson, who weighs 10,400 pounds, is only one of two elephants in the U.S. (the only one in a zoo) who breeds naturally (as opposed to artificial insemination). Thus far, Jackson has sired six offspring, with more on the way. By the way, the gestation period for an elephant is about 22 months.

ARTS, CULTURE, EDUCATION AND ENTERTAINMENT

An artistic success. An anatomical improbability. Photo by Kevin Cooke courtesy of the Pittsburgh Cultural Trust.

MUSIC

What touring Broadway production has had the longest run in Pittsburgh?

The Phantom of the Opera *ran from July 24 to September 5, 1993. Seventy-five performances attracted 210,000 fans. They paid a total of $11 million. One million went to the City of Pittsburgh in amusement taxes.*

John-Michael Tebelak wrote a master's thesis project at Carnegie Mellon University in 1971 that went on to become a Broadway musical. Name that musical.

Godspell.

He was born in Pittsburgh. He played the piano. He composed the song *Misty*. Who was he?

Erroll Garner.

Which internationally acclaimed jazz pianist, born in Duquesne, PA in 1905, created a revolutionary right-handed technique for improvising melodies on the piano?

Earl "Fatha" Hines.

Which Pittsburgh jazz singer was known as "Mr. B."?

Billy Eckstine. His first big hit Skylark, *was recorded with Earl "Fatha" Hines.*

Which nationally known jazz pianist, born in Pittsburgh, wrote the song *Pittsburgh*?

Ahmad Jamal. Jamal from East Liberty started to play professionally at age 11. His 1958 album, But Not for Me, *had sales of over a million. He was born as Fritz Jones in 1930.*

The University of Pittsburgh alma mater is sung to what melody?

Old Austrian Hymn, *which is the German national anthem. Pitt's* alma mater *lyrics were written by George M.P. Baird, a 1909 graduate. Another popular Pitt song,* Hail to Pitt, *goes back to 1910. Lester M. Taylor wrote the music and George M. Kirk wrote* Hail to Pitt's *lyrics.*

The gold record *The Rapper* was written and sung by what Pittsburgh area artist?

Donnie Iris from Beaver Falls. The Rapper sold more than a million copies and was number 2 on the Billboard *charts.*

The Rogers and Hart song *Blue Moon* written in 1934 was recorded by a Pittsburgh doo-wop group in 1961, and it stayed number one on *Billboard's* pop chart for 14 consecutive weeks. The group took its name from a French finger wave hairstyle that was popular at the time. What's the group's name?

The Marcels.

By day William Pollak is a technical writer at Carnegie Mellon University. By night he is a singer in a rock and roll band. What is Pollak's band/stage name?

Billy Price.

What was the name of the Canonsburg singing group which made *Shangri-La* a popular hit?

The Four Coins.

Which singer recorded the song *There's a Pawn Shop on the Corner in Pittsburgh, Pennsylvania*?

The now long forgotten Guy Mitchell, who died in 1998.

From the 1890s until now, the Pittsburgh Symphony has had only 13 people head the orchestra, either as conductors or "titled music directors." How many can you name? (Hint: One of them was married to actress Mia Farrow).

The easy selection is Farrow's husband, André Previn. He was in charge from 1976 – 1984. The others are Frederick Arch (1896-1898), Victor Herbert (1898-1904), Emil Paur (1904-1910), Antonio Modarelli (1930-1937), Otto Klemperer (1937-1938), Fritz Reiner (1938-1948), William Steinberg (1952-1976), Lorin Maazel (1987-1996), Maris Jansons (1997-2004), and the present day triumvirate that began in 2004 of Sir Andrew Davis, Yan Pascal Tortelier, and Marek Janowski.

This musical composer may have been born in Cleveland, Ohio (1924), but he spent his formative years in Aliquippa, PA (Beaver County) so Western Pennsylvanians consider him a native son. His father taught him how to play the flute and piccolo. He worked with Benny Goodman and Tex Beneke and attended Julliard. He's won twenty Grammy awards and four Academy Awards (18 nominations). His compositions include *The Pink Panther Theme*, *Peter Gunn*, *Love Theme from Romeo and Juliet*, and *Moon River*. Clearly, he's no clumsy Inspector Clouseau. Who is he?

Henry Mancini, who died on June 14, 1994.

Few Pittsburghers would know this jazz pianist and composer by her birth name: Mary Elfrieda Winn. She was born in Atlanta, Georgia in 1910 and moved to Pittsburgh by the age of five or six. She wrote and arranged music for the likes of Louis Armstrong, Benny Goodman, the Dorseys and Duke Ellington. She wrote *Zodiac Suite, Little Joe from Chicago, Cloudy, Walkin' and Swingin,' Steppin' Pretty* and *Bearcat Shuffle*. She became a fixture in New York's jazz society. After converting to Catholicism, she started to write jazz for sacred purposes. One of her works was performed at New York's Saint Patrick's Cathedral, another was commissioned by the Vatican. To Pittsburgh jazz fans, Mary Elfrieda Winn is better known as?

Mary Lou Williams.

Point Counterpoint II and the American Wind Symphony celebrate the Bicentennial in July, 1976 at Point State Park. Photo by Lou Malkin. Courtesy Carnegie Library of Pittsburgh.

What was the name of the barge owned by the American Wind Symphony that sailed on Pittsburgh's waterways and docked to play symphonic music at local river towns?

Point Counterpoint II. *The vessel sailed over 400,000 miles at an average speed of 6 mph, even going as far as Saint Petersburg, Russia. It went into drydock in 1996.*

How many appearances did the Beatles make in Pittsburgh?

Only one—September 14, 1964. They performed at the Civic Arena.

S he was born as Aliyah Rabia in the Homewood section of Pittsburgh on June 3, 1931. She studied music at Pittsburgh's Filion School of Music. After graduating from Pittsburgh's Westinghouse High School in 1948, this jazz singer left the city for Detroit in 1950. She was first discovered in a Harlem nightclub and from there she began performing in major cities in the U.S. and Canada. She was named *Down Beat*'s "most promising newcomer of the year 1955." Her biggest selling albums are *The Late, Late Show* and *Dynamic.* Pittsburgh jazz fans know her as?

Dakota Staton.

W hat local musical group took its name from the thorny bushes that grow in the Pittsburgh area?

The Jaggerz, popular in the 1970s, are named after the thorny "jagger" bushes. The group was originally the Jaggers, but that name belonged to another band. The Jaggerz best seller was The Rapper.

W hat 1950s doo-wop song starts "dom, dom, dom, dom, dom-dee-doobie dom"? What group recorded the song?

The song is Come Go With Me, *recorded by the Del Vikings. The group of five met in 1955 at an Air Force base near Pittsburgh.*

A number one song, *Moja Droga Ja Cie Kocham (Melody of Love),* was recorded by a Polish-American born in Canonsburg, PA. Who is this "Polish Prince" recording artist?

Bobby Vinton. Vinton graduated from Duquesne University in 1956 with a degree in musical composition. Some of his other hits include Roses Are Red, Blue Velvet, *and* Mr. Lonely. *Vinton now appears at the 1,000 seat Bobby Vinton Blue Velvet Theater in Branson, Missouri.*

Bruce Springsteen won a Grammy for best solo rock vocal performance in 2003 for *Code of Silence*. Springsteen co-wrote the song with a Pittsburgh rock and roller. Who is he?

He's Joe Grushecky who is in the local band, The Houserockers. *When he's not hanging out with Springsteen, Grushecky teaches developmentally-delayed children at a local school.*

Abdullah Ibn Buhaina died in 1990 after a very successful career as an American jazz drummer and band leader. He was born in Pittsburgh's Hill District in 1919. He played with Bill (another Pittsburgher) Eckstine's band as well as with Thelonious Monk and Miles Davis. In 1955 he started his own group, Jazz Messengers, which was usually a sextet. What is Abdullah Ibn Buhaina's birth name and how is he still known to many jazz fans?

Art Blakey.

Duke Ellington was better known than his Pittsburgh collaborator. But Ellington's musical partner, the composer of *Take the 'A' Train* and *Lush Life*, is still considered a jazz great. Who was the Duke's relatively anonymous collaborator?

Billy Strayhorn, who grew up in the Homewood-Brushton area. Strayhorn, alone or with Ellington, composed about 200 works.

Which well-known Pittsburgh born jazz tenor saxophonist recorded his biggest hit album, *Sugar*, with another Pittsburgher, George Benson? He also played in a band with Ray Charles. His other albums include: *Up at Minton's* and *Never Let Me Go*. Finally, there is the album *Stan the Man* _____. Fill in the name of this jazz great.

Stanley Turrentine.

The first concert held at Heinz Field took place on August 18, 2001. What group performed?

*NSYNC.

What musical group played the last concert held at Three Rivers Stadium?

*NSYNC in July, 2000.

What Pittsburgh rock group made its network television debut on *Late Night with David Letterman* on August 31, 2004?

The Clarks.

Ten years after this pop music star was born on Staten Island, New York to Irish and Ecuadorian parents, she sang the national anthem for the Pirates and Steelers. She lived in Wexford as a youngster and was part of the Mickey Mouse Club at age 12. Her first album, with the hit single *Genie In A Bottle* on it, came out in 1999. Her self-titled album hit #1 in the U.S. Her name?

Christina Aguilera.

Art and Architecture

Which architect, by himself or in collaboration with others, designed the following buildings: Soldiers and Sailors Hall (1907-1911), University Club (1923), City-County Building (1915-17), Rodef Shalom Temple (1906-07), Webster Hall (1925-26), University of Pittsburgh's Schenley Quadrangle (1922), Mellon Institute (1931-37), Grant Building (1927-30), Carnegie Mellon University's Margaret Morrison Hall (1906-07)?

Henry Hornbostel. Not bad for a partial list.

View of southeast porch at Kentuck Knob in Chalk Hill, PA. Designed by Frank Lloyd Wright for I. N. and Bernardine Hagan, it was completed in 1956. Photo by Jack E. Boucher, 1986, for the Historic American Building Survey. Library of Congress, HABS PA, 26-Chalk, 12.

The Frank Lloyd Wright-designed Fallingwater in Fayette County has an international reputation. About ten miles from Fallingwater is another Wright home. What is its name?

Kentuck Knob. This less well-known Wright home was completed in 1956 for the I. N. Hagan family, Uniontown ice cream manufacturers. Kentuck Knob is now owned by Londoner Lord Peter Palumbo and is open to the public.

How many people visited the Frank Lloyd Wright-designed Fallingwater in 2005?

127,536.

Which two internationally known architects, closely identified with the Bauhaus school in Germany, designed a house on Woodland Road in Shadyside?

Walter Gropius and Marcel Breuer. The Bauhaus was started in Weimar in 1919 and at one time was headed by Gropius. Breuer was on the faculty.

A visitor to the Agnes R. Katz Plaza at Seventh and Penn in the Cultural District may stop and perform what highly improbable anatomical act?

Sit on an eye. The plaza's benches are granite "eyeballs." They were designed by internationally known sculptor Louise Bourgeois.

Pittsburgh's first art gallery opened in 1832. What is the name/location?

J. J. Gillespie Gallery was first located at 6 Wood Street, downtown, replacing Albree's Novelty Shop at that location. After a fire in 1845, Gillespie's moved to 86 Wood Street. It is still in business today in McMurray, PA. The "J. J." is for John Jones.

Which Pittsburgh artist painted sixty-five portraits for the cover of *Time* magazine?

Henry Koerner. His cover subjects have included Maria Callas, John Cheever and Barbra Streisand.

North Carolina-born artist Selma Burke lived in Pittsburgh between 1968 and 1976. For what did she achieve national fame, albeit before she became a Pittsburgher?

Burke designed the bust of Franklin Delano Roosevelt that appears on every dime, unveiling the full-size model for the dime in 1945.

At the intersection of Second Avenue and Ross Street underneath the Boulevard of the Allies is a mural titled, *Legends of Pittsburgh Baseball*. Featured are 14 players. How many can you name?

From left to right they are: Kiki Cuyler, Ralph Kiner, Fred Clarke, Max Carey, Paul Waner, Lloyd Waner, Danny Murtaugh, Josh Gibson, Arky Vaughn, Willie Stargell, Pie Traynor (kneeling), Bill Mazeroski, Roberto Clemente and Honus Wagner.

There is more to Market Square than pigeons. On a building facing the Square and Forbes Avenue is a large mural and collage, *Regional Patterns*. What materials make up the artwork and what does the art portray?

The place has 20 restored molds used to make steel at USX's Duquesne Works. The molds represent the three rivers. Four panels on the piece simulate the quadrants of Market Square. Christopher Siefert and Yaming Di, graduates of CMU's art school, designed the mural. It was financed by various local foundations, corporations, and private sources.

Victor David Brenner designed *A Song to Nature*, the fountain near the entrance to the Carnegie Library in Oakland. Brenner is more famous for designing what common object? (Hint: A penny for your thoughts).

Brenner designed the Lincoln portrait that appears on a U.S. penny. He presented the design to President Theodore Roosevelt in 1909 on the centennial of Lincoln's birth.

MUSEUMS

When did the Three Rivers Arts Festival start? Who started it?
1960. The Junior Women's Committee of the Carnegie Museum of Art.

What is the size of the permanent collection at the Warhol Museum?

The museum has 4,000 objects and 610 time capsules in its permanent collection. The museum has 70,000 square feet of building space and 47,000 square feet of exhibition space.

At the Forbes Avenue entrance to the Carnegie museums are four large, sculpted figures symbolizing literature, music, art and science. Which historical figures in the sculptures depict the disciplines?

Shakespeare, Bach, Michelangelo and Galileo. The figures date back to 1907.

What United States national monuments did Pittsburgh's Carnegie Museum of Natural History help found?

The Dinosaur National Monument in Colorado and Utah was begun based on skeletons Carnegie paleontologists discovered there in the early 1900s. The Agate Fossil Beds National Monument in western Nebraska has its origins in the early 20th century also. Carnegie scientists discovered 15 million year old mammal fossils (horses, rhinos, pigs) in that location.

What is the name of the large dinosaur on the prowl in front of the Carnegie Museum on Forbes Avenue in Oakland and how big is he?

The dinosaur's name is "Dippy" and he is patterned after Diplodocus Carnegii. *Dippy is 85 feet in length and 18 feet high. Carnegie paleontologists found this specimen first. Its replica is now in museums all over the world, especially Europe. Andrew Carnegie gave the first replica to the King of England in 1905, already put together, too. The rather oddly costumed small model of a* Tyrannosaurus Rex *nearby is the result of a local fund-raiser.*

Andrew W. Mellon, Secretary of the Treasury, in his Washington, DC office on June 14, 1929. National Photo Company Collection, Herbert E. French, Library of Congress, LC-USZ62-52418.

Which ex-Pittsburghers as a family are the largest benefactors of the Washington, DC National Gallery of Art?

Andrew W. Mellon, and his children, Alisa Mellon Bruce, and Paul Mellon. They are considered founding benefactors.

Bugs are unwelcome guests at most buildings, but not at the Carnegie Museum of Natural History's section of invertebrate zoology. How many insects are in the Carnegie's collection?

Between 6 and 7 million prepared specimens, that is, specimens pinned or glued for display. There are another four and a half to five million unprepared specimens, which are mostly stored in alcohol. The Carnegie collection dates back to the 1860s.

The 1,000-foot French luxury liner *Normandy* (built for $60 million in 1935) may possibly be the most beautifully decorated ocean liner ever to sail. A New York collector purchased one of the Normandy's murals, *The Chariot of Aurora*, for $2.5 million in the 1980s. Where can you see the mural today?

The collector gave the 18-foot tall by 26-foot wide mural to the Carnegie Museum of Art and it is on display in the Scaife Galleries. The Normandy *was accidentally set on fire and eventually sold for scrap. She was in service for only four years.*

What area museum has one of the country's largest private collection of Meissen porcelain?

The Maridon Museum in Butler, Pennsylvania has over 300 Meissen pieces. (Meissen is a fine porcelain produced in Meissen, Germany; it is also referred to as Dresden china.) The museum's Asian collection has more than 400 artifacts.

The Carnegie museums (formerly the Carnegie Institute) had a once and only pressure wash cleaning in the 1990s. But a rectangular blotch of black on two walls remains to the rear of the music hall looking out on the Schenley Plaza. Why wasn't the building given a complete bath?

The remaining spot is a way to pay homage to the Institute's founder, Andrew Carnegie, and the city's industrial past when buildings routinely turned black from the soot clogging the air.

Which internationally known sculptor created the 466-inch high, Cor-Ten steel sculpture at the entrance to the Carnegie Museum of Art and what is the title of the piece?

Richard Serra. The piece is titled Carnegie. *It's dedicated to the memory of William Roesch, who was an executive at Jones and Laughlin Steel Corporation and at U.S. Steel.*

A bit of Tennessee (Williams) near Pittsburgh. Photo by Scott R. Becker. Courtesy of the Pennsylvania Trolley Museum.

Tennessee Williams is gone, but where can you evoke his memory by riding *A Streetcar Named Desire*?

At the Pennsylvania Trolley Museum in Washington, PA. In 1964, the museum bought the trolley from the City of New Orleans for one dollar when it became available. One reason it's here is because New Orleans and Pittsburgh are the only two cities in the U.S. that have a track gauge of five feet two and a half inches. (The gauge is the distance between the rails). New Orleans stopped running the Desire *in 1948.*

Students of the Bible and biblical archaeology can uncover some ancient finds (a wooden comb from a site near where the Dead Sea Scrolls were discovered, for example) at Pittsburgh's most undiscovered museum. What and where is the museum?

The James L. Kelso Bible Lands Museum at the Pittsburgh Theological Seminary in Highland Park.

There is only one Abraham Lincoln death mask in existence. Where is it?

The plaster of Paris mask is in Oakland's Soldiers and Sailors Museum and Memorial Hall on the ground floor in the West Hall.

Why is the Henry Clay Frick house in Pittsburgh's Point Breeze called *Clayton*?

Clayton *was Frick's middle name. His friends and family frequently addressed him by that name. Frick and his wife moved into* Clayton *in January, 1883; it was maintained long after her parents' deaths by their daughter, Helen Clay Frick, and is now a house museum open to the public.*

A motorist driving into this Point Breeze attraction could park alongside a 1914 Rolls Royce Silver Ghost, an 1898 Panhard Tonneau (possibly the first car in Pittsburgh), a 1909 Mercedes and a 1914 Ford Model T, to name a few. What is the name of this automotive fairyland?

The Frick Car and Carriage Museum at the Frick Art and Historical Center.

As a way to break the ice at a party, ask someone what was in the Senator John Heinz Regional History Center prior to its present use?

The Chautauqua Lake Ice Company stored thousands of tons of ice there. The building's walls are three feet thick and the wood beams supporting the floors are two feet wide. The ice came from the lake in southwestern New York and was shipped in by rail.

Sleep lovers may be a bit disappointed upon visiting the North Side's Mattress Factory. But not necessarily so. What will keep their eyes open?

A large, varied collection of newly created installation art. The Mattress Factory is an arts/educational/cultural organization that started in 1977. The art is created in the factory, and attracts international artists and visitors. At most, one half of the Factory's attendees come from outside the Pittsburgh region.

In 1901, Andrew Carnegie built a chateau in New York City on 91st Street between Fifth and Madison avenues. The building now houses what Smithsonian Institution Museum?

The Cooper-Hewitt Museum, the Smithsonian Institution's National Museum of Design.

THEATER AND THEATERS

Heinz Hall and the Benedum Center were movie theaters before they were renovated. What were the names of these theaters?

Heinz Hall was the Penn Theatre and the Benedum was the Stanley Theatre.

What Pittsburgh theater has the largest column-free backstage area in the U.S.?

The Benedum Center.

631-633 Liberty Avenue. Library of Congress, Historic American Buildings Survey, John A. Bertola, delineator, 1984. HABS PA, 2-PITBU, 40.

What kind of art was on display at the Art Cinema on Liberty Avenue before it was converted to the Harris Theater in 1995?

The 194-seat theater showed "adult" films or what some may have considered "porn" depending on one's viewpoint.

Pittsburgh had the world's theater premier showing motion pictures. Where was it located?

John P. Harris opened a nickelodeon in a building in the 400 block of Smithfield Street in downtown Pittsburgh in 1905. Opening day was a double bill featuring Poor But Honest *and* Baffled Burgler. *The present-day Harris Theater is named for him.*

The Heinz Hall Plaza at Sixth and Liberty is patterned after what vest-pocket park in New York City?

Paley Park on East 53rd Street. William S. Paley, founder of CBS, contributed the park to the city.

A discerning shopper in the market for a 20-foot high, two and a half ton (4,700 pound) chandelier with more than 50,000 crystals on it could find it where?

In the Benedum Center, downtown.

The world famous post-modern architect, Michael Graves, has works sprinkled throughout the United States. He's probably best known, however, for the products he designs for Target Stores, things like housewares, appliances, office supplies and electronics. What building did he design in Pittsburgh? (Beware! It is bigger than a tchotchke).

The O'Reilly Theater, which opened in 1999.

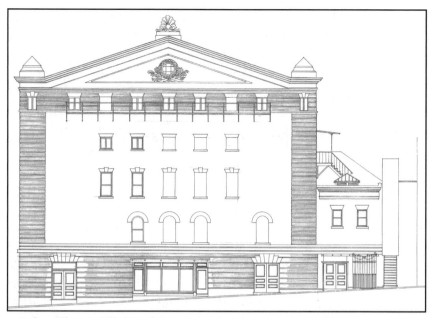

Fulton Theater. Library of Congress, Historic American Buildings Survey, Roger S. Gallet, delineator, 1967. HABS PA, 2-PITBU, 40.

The building now housing the Byham Theater on Sixth Street was what kind of a theater when it opened on Halloween night in 1904?

> *The Gayety Theater staged live vaudeville and "refined burlesque" productions. The building became a movie theater, the Fulton, in 1930. The Byham opened in 1995.*

The O'Reilly Theater has what kind of stage: a) proscenium; b) thrust; c) in the round?

> *b) Thrust.*

What was the first performance staged at the O'Reilly Theater?

> *The world premier of August Wilson's* King Hedley II.

What was the first entertainment/musical event to take place in the Civic Arena? What is the arena's attendance record?

The Ice Capades kicked things off on September 22, 1961. The first musical act was Judy Garland on October 19, 1961. She sold out with 12,365 fans (the Arena's original capacity); Fats Domino appeared next on October 20, 1961. He drew 9,385 fans. Johnny Mathis appeared on October 31, 1961. The attendance record is 18,150 for a World Wide Wrestling show in January 1999.

Gerome Ragni was born in Carnegie, PA (it's not clear what year) and after a hitch in the Air Force he moved to New York where he became an actor. He also loved music. He starred in and co-wrote the lyrics to a Broadway musical that opened in April, 1968. The show was controversial in its celebration of drugs, anti-war activity, and nudity. Some of the show's songs include *Aquarius*, *Easy to Be Hard*, and *Good Morning, Starshine*. What was the musical?

It was Hair. Hair *closed in July, 1972 after 1,742 performances. The cast also included Melba Moore and Diane Keaton. Ragni died in 1991.*

MOVIES

Actor Paul Newman starred in a 1970s film about hockey, part of which was filmed in nearby Johnstown. What was the name of the film?

Slap Shot. *In the movie, the town was called Charleston.*

What is the name of the first movie filmed in Pittsburgh and when was it filmed?

Various parts of The Perils of Pauline *were filmed here in 1914.*

Actors Michael Douglas and Tobey Maguire came to Pittsburgh to film *Wonder Boys*, based on a novel written by a University of Pittsburgh graduate who majored in English. Who wrote *Wonder Boys*?

Michael Chabon, who graduated from Pitt in 1984 (summa cum laude). Wonder Boys *was his second novel. His first,* The Mysteries of Pittsburgh, *was written for Chabon's master's thesis at University of California, Irvine.*

No intricate thought process needed to answer this question, just a basic instinct. Which movie actress born in Meadville, PA (1958) and educated at Edinboro (PA) University starred in *Total Recall* with Arnold Schwarzenegger, in *Casino* with Robert De Niro, and *Basic Instinct* with Michael Douglas?

Sharon Stone. For her role in Casino, *Stone earned an Academy Award nomination.*

In what 1942 movie do both John Wayne and Randolph Scott fall in love with Marlene Dietrich?

Pittsburgh. *In the movie, Wayne's nickname is "Pittsburgh." After Wayne ditches his bride-to-be on the night of the wedding and tries to rekindle an affair with Dietrich, she slaps him in the face.*

Photographed, edited, co-scripted and directed in Pittsburgh, mostly by Pittsburghers, this 1968 movie, which cost just $114,000 to make, has been called "one of the most influential horror films ever made" and "the best horror movie ever made." What's its title and who was its now famous producer/director?

The Night of the Living Dead *was produced and directed by George Romero.*

Which well-known Pittsburgh boxer was the star of the 1941 movie, *The Pittsburgh Kid*?

Billy Conn. In the movie, Conn plays a boxer facing a murder charge. But, all ends well.

Which Pittsburgh-born actor showcased his talent by singin' in the rain? He need not be embarrassed by his dancin', either.

Gene Kelly was born in Pittsburgh on August 23, 1912 and died in Beverly Hills, CA on February 2, 1996. He starred in Singin' in the Rain *in 1952. Kelly graduated from Peabody High School in Pittsburgh's East End and the University of Pittsburgh with a degree in economics. He went to Hollywood in 1941 right from Broadway where he appeared in* Pal Joey. *His name is up in lights at the Kelly-Strayhorn Theater in Pittsburgh's East Liberty neighborhood.*

A list of some of the movies this Pittsburgh actor has appeared in may be enough to figure out his identity: *Annie Hall* (1977; he had only a few lines), *Invasion of the Body Snatchers* (1978), *The Big Chill* (1983), *The Fly* (1986), *Jurassic Park* (1993), *The Lost World: Jurassic Park* (1997), and *Independence Day* (1996). Who is he?

Jeff Goldblum, who was born in Whitaker Borough, Allegheny County in October, 1952. In high school Goldblum studied art at the Carnegie Museum and acting at the Kresge Theater at Carnegie Mellon. He moved to New York City when he was 17. One of his lesser known talents is his ability to wiggle his ears one at a time.

He was born in Pittsburgh in 1902 and eventually became a Hollywood mogul. He brought Ingrid Bergman to America and produced *Gone With The Wind*. Who was he?

David O. Selznick. Selznick also signed Pittsburgher Gene Kelly to his first movie contract.

The role of the Riddler, Batman's nemesis, was played by this Pittsburgh-born actor in the 1960s television show *Batman*. In 2002, he appeared on Broadway as George Burns in *Goodnight Gracie*, which ran for about a year. In between, he did impressions of Jackie Gleason, Burt Lancaster, James Cagney, and others, appearing in television and in Las Vegas. Who left so many impressions?

It was Frank Gorshin, who was born in 1933 and died in 2005. Gorshin graduated from Pittsburgh's Peabody High School and attended Carnegie Tech for two years.

The Written Word

There are only 250 facsimiles of Chaucer's *Canterbury Tales* in existence in the world. One is in Pittsburgh. Where?

On the ground floor of Hillman Library at the University of Pittsburgh. Pitt paid $16,000 for it in 2001. The facsimile is in the glass case in the Hillman recording room. The reading room's name is The Cup and Chaucer.

What is the University of Pittsburgh Press's all-time best selling book?

Out of this Furnace *by Thomas Bell. It is a novel about three generations of an immigrant Slovak family working in Braddock's steel mills. The book has sold over 169,000 copies.*

Does Harry Potter have a Pittsburgh area ancestor?

With a little imagination the answer is yes. The Harry Potter *series is published in the United States by* Scholastic. *On October 22, 1920 M. R. "Robbie" Robinson started the Scholastic Publishing Company in his hometown of Wilkinsburg, Pennsylvania. Today the company, now in New York and headed by the founder's son, has sales of over $2 billion and publishes over 35 classroom magazines with a circulation of about 35 million students in grades K-12, plus 40 million parents.*

Who is the most famous person to ever read poetry at Pittsburgh's International Poetry Forum?

Surely, it is Grace Kelly. Then again, Queen Noor appeared in June 2005. Does a queen outrank a mere princess in this context?

Which Pittsburgh-born author received the Pulitzer Prize for Biography in 1993?

David McCullough. It was for Truman. *McCullough also received a Pulitzer in 2002 for* John Adams.

LIBRARIES

How many free libraries did Andrew Carnegie donate to the world?

2,509. He donated $56,162,622 for construction of the libraries, but nothing for their upkeep.

How many libraries did Andrew Carnegie's philanthropy build in the United States?

1,679. They were built within 1,412 communities.

How many volumes are in the University of Pittsburgh's twenty-eight libraries?

There are about 4.5 million books and around 35,000 subscriptions (magazines, journals).

How many books are circulated through the entire Carnegie Library of Pittsburgh system each year?

In 2004, the figure was 3,256,853.

The Carnegie Library in Braddock is the first in the United States. Courtesy of Braddock's Field Historical Society.

Where did Andrew Carnegie build his first public library?

In Braddock in 1889. The building is still functioning as a library.

What are the ages of the Carnegie Library of Pittsburgh's oldest and youngest card holders?

A few are a week or so old. The oldest is 98 years old. There is also a 96 year old card carrying member.

How many books are in the entire Carnegie Library of Pittsburgh system?

2,315,602 books.

What are the most frequently asked questions at the Carnegie Library's Ready Reference Center?

1. Who are the tallest and shortest presidents?

2. Who are the members of the U.S. Supreme Court?

3. When was the "H" added to Pittsburgh?

4. What are the words to the Twelve Days of Christmas?

What ranks as possibly the weirdest question ever received at the Carnegie Library of Pittsburgh's Ready Reference Center?

"Is Mount Rushmore natural or man-made?"

The Carnegie Library of Pittsburgh is usually in the business of dispensing books to its patrons, but once in its history it handed out an honorary high school diploma to a ninth grade dropout, no less. Who received the library's honorary high school diploma?

Playwright August Wilson picked up a degree from the Carnegie in 1989. After Wilson left Gladstone Junior High School at the age of fifteen, he pursued his education at the Oakland branch of the library.

COLLEGES & UNIVERSITIES

What was the first school in the United States to offer a bachelor's degree in bagpipes?

Carnegie Mellon University. The first degree was granted in May, 1996. CMU also offered the first undergraduate degree in drama in 1917. It was also the first school to offer a PhD in robotics in 1989.

When they were founded in 1878 and 1787 respectively, Duquesne University and the University of Pittsburgh had different names. What were their original names?

Duquesne was founded as the Pittsburgh Catholic College of the Holy Ghost. Pitt began as the Pittsburgh Academy.

What does the log cabin type structure on the Forbes Avenue side of the Cathedral of Learning symbolize?

It is a replica of a campus building that existed at the time of Pitt's founding in 1787.

Ron Tappy, a professor of Bible and archaeology at the Pittsburgh Theological Seminary, was in Israel in July 2005 directing an archaeological dig when he came across something old—something very old. What did Tappy find?

Tappy discovered a limestone boulder that goes back to 10th century B.C.E. (King Solomon's time). Appearing on the boulder are markings that possibly are letters from the Hebrew alphabet. The stone weighs 40 pounds and may contain the alphabet from which all other alphabets in the ancient world are derived. The discovery is about 20 miles south of Jerusalem in Tel Zayit.

How many nationality rooms are there at the University of Pittsburgh?

26, all of them located in the Cathedral of Learning. The rooms were started in 1938, and the first rooms were Swedish, Scottish, German, Russian and Early American. The most recent room is Indian and was added in 2000.

What local university has the largest endowment?

The University of Pittsburgh's endowment reached $1.4 billion at the end of 2004. That is up from about $485 million in 1995. Carnegie Mellon University's endowment is about $815 million.

They are used in e-mail all over the world now, but Carnegie Mellon University researcher, Scott Fahlman, typed the first one on September 19, 1982. What are they?

Emoticons. The first one he posted was "smiley" or :-).

What is the oldest women's liberal arts college in the U.S. west of the Alleghenies?

Chatham College, which was founded in 1869 as the Pennsylvania Female College.

Dr. A. Lester Pierce brought his orchestra from Saint Edward's University in Austin, Texas to a local university in 1937. That orchestra, which plays ethnic music, is still here performing about 80 times a year all over America. What did Dr. Pierce import from Texas?

The Duquesne University Tamburitzans, all of whom are undergraduate students.

Carlow University is named after a town in what country?

Ireland. Carlow was founded by the Sisters of Mercy, an Irish order. The Sisters of Mercy came to Pittsburgh in 1843. In 1894 the sisters bought 13 acres of land on which Carlow now sits. Finally, on September 24, 1929, Carlow (originally named Mount Mercy) opened, weeks before the Great Depression. Sisters Irenaeus Dougherty and Regis Grace were the school's founders. Mount Mercy became Carlow in 1969.

Indians helped supply a name for what local university?

Slippery Rock. Presumably the Indians had trouble navigating a nearby creek.

FLORA AND FAUNA AND THE GREAT OUTDOORS

How many state parks are in Allegheny County?

At the present time, two—Point State Park, plus there is a 43-acre undeveloped park on the Allegheny Islands in the Allegheny River about 14 miles upstream from the Point.

How many telephone calls seeking information are received by the Phipps Conservatory's Garden Place Greenline each year?

The Greenline gets about 4,000 calls a year. Most callers want to know how the changes in weather or temperature will affect their plants.

Pittsburgh Voyager *plies the three rivers at the Point. Courtesy Pittsburgh Voyager.*

Pittsburgh Voyager is a nonprofit group offering educational adventures on Pittsburgh's rivers for area students, teachers, and community groups. The adventure takes place on Voyager's fleet of three boats. Two of the three boats, *Voyager* and *Discovery* had a military use before the federal government donated them to Pittsburgh Voyager. What was their original use by the U.S. Navy?

The Navy used the 78.7-foot boats to train personnel in navigation and ship handling. Discovery *was built in 1958,* Voyager *in 1966. In 1993,* Voyager *was placed on a barge with a specially made crane and towed to Pittsburgh by the way of the Ohio and Mississippi rivers.* Discovery, *in May, 1997, sailed from the Tombigbee Waterway in Alabama under its own power to Pittsburgh. The boats' hulls are made of Douglas Fir and Alaskan Cedar.* Voyager *can handle 49 passengers and* Discovery, *40. They are docked on Pittsburgh's North Shore.*

Barges are a common sight on the Monongahela River, but dragon boats? When do they sail on the Mon?

During the Pittsburgh Dragon Boat Festival held in September. The dragon is a national symbol in China and at one time served as the badge of the royal family. There is a big dragon boat festival in China's Guangdong Province each year.

How many different kinds of plants are in Phipps Conservatory's permanent collection?

Around 5,000. The figure varies due to acquisition and removals.

How many buffalo roam in Allegheny County's South Park?

Nine.

In the City of Pittsburgh, which is bigger: Frick Park or Schenley Park? (Hint: It's pretty close.)

It is Frick with 456.8 acres. Schenley has 456 acres. Highland Park has 425 acres for a not-too-distant third.

How many people visited Point State Park in 2004?

An estimated 2.6 million. Point State Park is the third most visited state park behind Presque Isle and Pymatuning.

Money, Money, Money

How much money did Allegheny County organizations receive from the National Endowment for the Arts in 2006?

$193,000. The money went to nine different groups: The Mattress Factory ($50,000), Children's Museum of Pittsburgh ($38,000), Pittsburgh Opera ($35,000), Pittsburgh Ballet Theater ($10,000), Pittsburgh Dance Alloy ($10,000), Pittsburgh International Children's Theater and Festival ($10,000), Pittsburgh Cultural Trust ($15,000), Squonk Opera ($20,000), and the Creative Nonfiction Foundation ($5,000). In 2004, the NEA gave $152,100 to eight groups. In 1999, however, eighteen local groups received $623,500 from the NEA.

From a dollar and cents standpoint, what is the economic impact of the arts locally?

Based on a 1998 survey, the arts community pumps $170 million dollars directly into Allegheny County's economy.

How many people visit Allegheny County each year and how much money do they leave behind?

There were 10.2 million overnight guests in 2003. But, according to the latest impact study, all visitors—both overnighters and day-trippers—spent $3.6 billion.

The Miscellaneous and the Merely Strange

What does the Mortality Club of Allegheny County do for fun?

Its members try to anticipate when the next famous person will go to his or her final reward. The club has plenty of actuaries and insurance people as members, so there is a degree of professionalism in this ghoulish past-time.

Which Pittsburgh native and Carnegie Mellon University graduate demonstrated a superior knowledge of Shakespeare on *The $64,000 Question* and played Agent 99 in the TV series *Get Smart?*

Barbara Feldon.

On average, how many visitors drop in at the Greater Pittsburgh Convention and Visitors Bureau information booth at Gateway Center each year?

28,000+.

In terms of number of attendees, what's the biggest convention ever held in Pittsburgh?

The National Rifle Association Convention in April 2004 drew 60,000 people.

From what European countries do the terms "nebby" (nosey), and "yinz" (you all) originate?

Scotland and Ireland. There's a chance "redd up" as in "redd up the house" has the same origin.

Which of these statements about Kennywood's Grand Carousel is *not* accurate?

1. Construction of the carousel started in 1926, and Kennywood bought it in 1927 for $25,000.
2. The carousel has a 54-foot diameter.
3. It has 50 jumping horses, 14 stationary horses, 4 chariots, a tiger, and a lion.
4. A 1916 Wurlitzer organ supplies the carousel's music.

All statements are accurate.

Today, it is formally known as the Brentwood Civic Center (Brentwood Borough, Allegheny County). Previously it was the Brentwood Park Shelter, but more informally it was named after the disc jockey, Jack Sullivan, who hosted teen dances there in the '50s and '60s. What was the shelter's informal name?

Sully's. Sullivan drew thousands of teens from the Carrick, Brentwood and Baldwin areas. Patti Page, Vic Damone, and The Four Aces, among others, appeared at Sully's.

Just Ducky Tours explores Pittsburgh by land and water. The tours are done in what kind of vehicle?

They are conducted in fully restored World War II amphibious vehicles known as DUKWs. In water, DUKWs are steered by their front wheels and a rudder, which is connected to the steering gear. Originally, DUKWs were expected to last only 90 days. DUKW? That's US Army Code: D (1942); U (amphibian); K (all wheel drive); W (dual rear axles).

Since 1843, when the Roman Catholic Church set up its first diocese in the Pittsburgh area, eleven bishops have administered the diocese. How many of the eleven were born in the Pittsburgh area?

Three. The first was Bishop J.F. Regis Canevin, who served from 1904-1920. He was born in Westmoreland County and Canevin High School is named after him. Bishop Vincent Leonard served from 1969-1983; and Donald Wuerl became bishop in 1988. Leonard and Wuerl were born in Pittsburgh.

PLACES OF INTEREST

Meeting "under the clock" presented a challenge on August 14, 1945—V-J Day. Courtesy Carnegie Library of Pittsburgh.

What is the diameter of Kaufmann's clock? When was it built?

The bronze timepiece is six feet in diameter and was built around 1888. The Kaufmann brothers moved into the present location at Smithfield Street and Fifth Avenue in 1878. The structure at that location was built in 1913. Federated Department stores brought Kaufmann's in 2005; it is being re-vamped as Macy's. Meet you under the Macy's clock???

The Margaret Morrison building at Carnegie Institute of Technology (now Carnegie Mellon University) was built in 1907. Who was Margaret Morrison?

In a gesture of possible Oedipal significance, Andrew Carnegie named the building for his mother.

At the Pittsburgh International Airport, what is the distance between the landside and airside terminals and how long does it take the people mover to travel between them?

The people mover travels 2,500 feet between the terminals in 63 seconds. It can move 13,200 passengers an hour.

What is the oldest existing skyscraper in downtown Pittsburgh?

The 15-story Park Building at Fifth and Wood was built in 1896.

On what fashionable street were The Gazebo, Fox's, The Encore, and the Hollywood Social Club located?

Walnut Street in Shadyside.

The simple plaque reads: "In memory of those who lived and died on our streets. We believe you are no longer cold, hungry, lonely or frightened. May you watch over us from a warm, caring home above." Where is the plaque and what does it represent?

The plaque is in downtown Pittsburgh at the intersection of Grant Street and Fort Pitt Boulevard, underneath a parkway ramp. The plaque and 70 smaller ones, with individualized names, memorialize the homeless who died on Pittsburgh streets. The first individualized plaque, with a 1989 date, is for Sarge, no last name. Operation Safety Net, a volunteer, nonprofit group that provides medical care and social services for Pittsburgh's homeless, placed the plaques.

Cathedral of Learning: What's missing from this photo? Courtesy of the University of Pittsburgh.

Pitt's 42-story Cathedral of Learning is missing a floor. Which one and why?

The 39th Floor. One theory is that the Gulf Building, which was owned by the Mellon family, had 39 floors and they didn't want any other building to have the same number of floors at the time the Cathedral was being built.

How high is the Cathedral of Learning at the University of Pittsburgh?

It is 42 stories, 535 feet high. Construction of the building started in September 1926 and finished in 1937.

When did Gimbels and the Joseph Horne department stores close their downtown Pittsburgh locations?

Gimbels closed on September 13, 1986. It moved into its building on Sixth Avenue in 1913.

Horne's moved into its Penn Avenue and Stanwix Street location in 1893. Horne's was sold to Lazarus in 1994 and the Stanwix Street store was closed on December 24, 1995.

Much of the French and Indian War (1763-1755) was fought in Western Pennsylvania. What incident was thought to start the war as well as the Seven Years' War in Europe, and what famous American was involved in the incident?

The war was triggered by the killing of Joseph Coulon, Sieur de Jumonville, and nine other Frenchmen in what is now Fayette County. The French were carrying diplomatic credentials and instructions to find the English and discuss making peace. Initially, George Washington was held responsible for the killings but eventually a Seneca Indian, Tanacharison (Half-king), was to blame.

Of the massacre Voltaire would write "a cannon shot fired in America could give the world the signal that set Europe in a blaze." The Seven Years' War (the French and Indian War was part of the larger, European war) had started and 853,000 soldiers would die.

How big is the Bayer sign on Mount Washington?

It is 30 feet, six inches high and 226 feet, six inches long. The letters for the sign require more than a mile of neon tubing.

R ed Pole was a chief of the Shawnee Indians. He died in Pittsburgh in 1797. Nathaniel Bedford was Pittsburgh's first physician. He died in 1818. Alfred Irenaeus Hopkins is the only Pittsburgher to serve as the ecclesiastical head of the Episcopal Church in America. He died in 1830. Where are these folks buried in downtown Pittsburgh?

At Trinity Cathedral's Burial Ground on Sixth Avenue. Native Americans were burying people at this site before any Europeans arrived. The spot was called a tumulus (burying ground) and at one time over 4,000 persons were buried there.

A t what local school was the Salk vaccine tested?

On June 12, 1952, Jonas Salk started his testing at the D. T. Watson Home for Crippled Children in Leetsdale. Children already recovering from polio were inoculated. So were staff members. The facility is now called the Watson Institute. David Thompson Watson was a local lawyer who represented the United States government in a land dispute with Russia over Alaskan land.

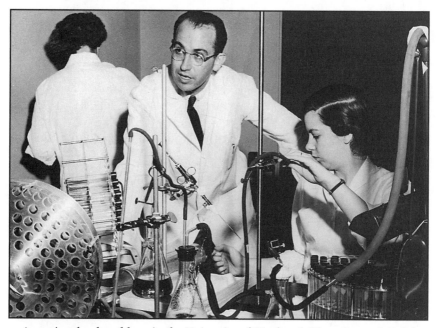

A vaccine developed here in the University of Pittsburgh Virus Research Lab has saved lives for generations. Courtesy Carnegie Library of Pittsburgh.

In 1943, as Pittsburghers went off to fight in World War II, some people had to leave pets behind. What group was started in that year to find homes to care for left behind pets?

It was Animal Friends. The pets, originally, were taken to private homes. In the 1960s Animal Friends built a shelter in the city's Strip District. In 2006 Animal Friends moved to a new shelter in Ohio Township.

Catherine and William Booth started the Salvation Army in London, England in 1865. Where and when was the first Salvation Army Worship and Service Center established in Pittsburgh?

On the North Side in 1880.

How high is the Commons Room at the University of Pittsburgh's Cathedral of Learning?

It measures 175-by-128 feet and is 52 feet high.

What is downtown's tallest building?

The USX Tower. It is 841 feet high.

What is the maximum height the Point State Park Fountain can reach?

It has gone as high as 150 feet. The fountain cost three million dollars and was dedicated on August 30, 1974.

How much did it cost to build Point State Park?

About $17 million. That is exclusive of highway connections.

What does a blinking blue light on top of the Gulf Building signify?

Fair weather. A blinking red light forecasts precipitation.

What does the beacon on top of the Grant Building, in downtown Pittsburgh, spell at night?

P-I-T-T-S-B-U-R-G-H. The building has been sending the signal since it opened in 1927 and it is visible for up to 125 miles.

What is possibly the longest Victorian architectural-style street in America?

Carson Street on the South Side of Pittsburgh. The area on Carson Street is between South 9th and South 25th streets. That section of Carson Street has three historic destinations: National Register of Historic Places (1983); City Historic District (1993); "Great American Main Street" by the National Trust for Historic Preservation (1996).

When was the only time a Pittsburgh building was damaged by a terrorist bombing?

On June 13, 1974, a bomb went off in the Gulf Building 18 minutes after a telephone call from someone claiming to be a member of the radical group, Weather Underground. There were no injuries. Presumably Gulf was targeted because the company was involved with colonial Portugal in Angola, Africa.

What was the name of the supper club located at the old Greater Pittsburgh International Airport?

The Horizon Room.

What do the Allegheny County Court House and the old city hall in Toronto, Canada have in common?

Toronto's old city hall is patterned after the Allegheny County Court House designed by H. H. Richardson. Toronto's building is smaller and its tower is not centered, as is the case with the Allegheny County Court House. Toronto's building was designed by Canadian E. J. Lennox.

What is the oldest building, of any kind, that is still standing in Allegheny County?

The honor goes to the Fort Pitt Blockhouse in Point State Park. The blockhouse was built in 1764.

Which internationally known architect, based in Chicago, designed the Frick Building, the Oliver Building and the Pennsylvania Station, all in downtown Pittsburgh?

D. H. Burnham, planner of the 1893 World's Columbian Exposition of 1893 on the shores of Lake Michigan and architect of master plans for Washington, DC, Chicago, San Francisco and Manila.

What is the connection between World War II submarine warfare and the county of Allegheny's wave pools?

To aid in submarine construction, Germany built large pools of water and used fans to churn the water, simulating ocean waves. The method to test submarine models is the same method the county uses to make its "wave pools."

What is the present location of the four proud bronze sphinxes that once guarded the now demolished Syria Mosque in Oakland?

They are at the side and front entrances of the newly built Syria Mosque located in Harmar Township, Allegheny County.

How many columns does Oakland's Mellon Institute have and how high are they? How many of the building's stories are underground?

There are 62 columns (all in the Ionic style) on the Institute's four sides. One-half of the building—nine stories—is underground. The columns are made of limestone from a quarry in the state of Indiana. Each column weighs nearly 60 tons and has an average diameter of five feet by 9 inches at the base and four feet by 11 inches at the neck. Including the base and capital, the columns are 40 feet, 11 inches high.

How big is a jail cell at the $142 million Allegheny County Jail on Second Avenue downtown? How big were the cells at the old, historic Allegheny County Jail on Grant Street?

The cells in the new jail are 84 square feet. The old jail had various sized cells. Some were around 47 square feet, others were a little over 46 square feet.

What is the Pittsburgh region's biggest cemetery in acres? Which one has the most people buried in it?

Jefferson Memorial in Allegheny County has 350 acres (including 7 miles of road). There are 69,000 people buried in Jefferson, which was named after Thomas Jefferson. The cemetery is mainly in Pleasant Hills with parts of it in Jefferson Borough and South Park Township. Allegheny Cemetery in the Lawrenceville section of Pittsburgh has 130,000 people buried in it. That's more than one-third of the city's population. Allegheny is exactly 300 acres in size.

Traditionally, what is Kennywood's most highly-attended day?

It's usually the last Thursday or Friday in August when people use leftover tickets before the park closes for the season. Each day averages about 18,000 patrons.

What religious sect with millions of members worldwide started in Pittsburgh in the 1870s?

Charles Taze Russell, a haberdasher from Allegheny City (now Pittsburgh's North Side), founded the Jehovah's Witnesses in Pittsburgh, although the headquarters is now located in Brooklyn.

After whom is Pittsburgh named?

In 1758, when General John Forbes took the area from the French, he named it after William Pitt, Earl of Chatham. At the time, Pitt was England's secretary of state for war. He was also known as Pitt the Elder to distinguish him from his son, Pitt the Younger.

Since 1981 (when the first transplant took place), how many transplants have been performed at the University of Pittsburgh Medical Center?

More than 12,000. The organs include hearts, lungs, kidneys, small bowels, pancreata, and livers. There are also combinations of transplants: heart/lung, double lung, heart/liver, kidney/pancreas, to name a few. In 2004, UPMC performed 265 liver transplants, 192 kidney transplants, and 39 heart transplants. UPMC's doctors have performed over 6,000 liver transplants, more than any other transplant center in the world.

The now defunct Duquesne Brewery on Pittsburgh's South Side had a "Have a Duke" functional clock on the side of its headquarters building. Subsequent clock advertisers were Stroh's Beer and WTAE-TV. At its broadest point, how big is the clock and whose face is now on it?

The clock is sixty feet wide or twice the size of London's Big Ben. It is now graced by the Equitable Gas name.

The USS Requin *submarine on patrol at the Carnegie Science Center. Courtesy of the Carnegie Science Center.*

The submarine USS *Requin* is docked on the Allegheny River near the Carnegie Science Center. What does the word "requin" mean and is the submarine longer or shorter than a football field?

Requin *is French for "sand shark." The sub is 11 feet, 8 inches longer than a football field.*

Where was the first proposed site for the Civic Arena?

Near Pittsburgh's Highland Park in the city's East End. The proposed site included most of the estate of Richard King Mellon's uncle. The estate, on North Negley Avenue, once housed a city office, but is now privately owned. It was known as King Center.

In March 1936, a major flood hit Pittsburgh. The high-water mark of that flood, 46 feet, is commemorated by a plaque on a downtown Pittsburgh building. On what building is this plaque?

Penn Avenue Place (the old Horne's Department Store) located at Penn and Stanwix.

The exterior of the Andy Warhol Museum on Pittsburgh's North Side is covered entirely with what material?

A cream-colored terra cotta.

Where was the first synagogue in the city of Pittsburgh?

In a rented room at the corner of Penn Avenue and Sixth Street in downtown Pittsburgh. The year was 1848 and the synagogue was Shaare Shamayim.

How high is the rotunda inside the Union Trust Building now known as Two Mellon Center?

130 feet. It rises through 11 stories.

What does "Coraopolis" mean?

"Cora" means beautiful; "opolis" means metropolitan city.

How big is the tree Duquesne Light installs each Christmas season at Point State Park?

It is 78 feet, 3 3/8 inches with a 4-feet, 6-inch star for a total of 82 feet 9 3/8 inches. It has 6,000 lights.

How many windows are in the USX Tower?

About 11,000.

Former Pittsburgh Pirates broadcaster, Bob Prince, had a nickname for the infield at Forbes Field. What was it?

"Alabaster Plaster."

Where did Lawrence Welk's bubbles first float to the surface?

In the 1940s, a William Penn Hotel engineer placed an electric fan in front of a pie pan filled with soap bubble liquid. Welk liked the effects and it became his trademark.

Where was the Maurice Salad created?

At the William Penn Hotel in downtown Pittsburgh in 1945. It is named after bandleader Maurice Spitalny who performed there.

What 52-foot, 11-inch object came down from the sky on 4:12 p.m. on January 31, 1956 a mile to a mile and a half downriver from the Homestead High Level Bridge (now the Homestead Grays Bridge) on the Monongahela River and has never been found?

A USAF B-25 bomber. Serial number 44-29125.

How tall is the mast on top of Fifth Avenue Place?

178 feet or about 13 stories. The mast is actually 12 sided and not round. It can sway up to 3 feet in any direction.

How many worms are consumed each week by the birds at the National Aviary on Pittsburgh's North Side?

About 60,000 mealworms are eaten.

How many different species of birds are at the National Aviary?

Nearly 200.

How many stained glass windows are in the University of Pittsburgh's Heinz Memorial Chapel?

There are 36 stained glass windows in the chapel (23 in the chapel's main body). The windows depict 319 famous figures. The chapel's four transept windows, which depict courage, tolerance, temperance, and truth, are 73 feet high and each one contains more than 25,000 pieces of glass.

What area hotel has the most rooms?

The Pittsburgh Hilton and Towers at Gateway Center with 712 rooms.

Since it was built in 1938, how many couples have been married at the University of Pittsburgh's Heinz Memorial Chapel?

A rough estimate is 13,000 couples. About 200 weddings a year take place there.

Thousands of motorists and pedestrians pass the intersection of Grant Street and the Boulevard of the Allies daily without paying much attention to their surroundings. At the intersection where the Boulevard begins to form a ramp are two columns. What objects are on top of the columns?

On top of the columns are granite American eagles clasping globes. The columns were designed by sculptor Frank Vittor. The two-mile boulevard was dedicated on Armistice Day 1922 to the people who had a hand in bringing World War I to a conclusion.

The Vietnam Veterans monument in Pittsburgh's Clemente Park depicts five statues underneath a chapel-like shell. The shell is an inverted hibiscus pod. What does the pod symbolize in Asian culture?

Re-birth and regeneration.

How big is the Christmas tree decoration on the side of the Penn Avenue Place (the former Horne's Department Store) in downtown Pittsburgh and located at Penn and Stanwix?

It is 100 feet high. At its base it is 68 feet wide. The tree contains 1,953 light bulbs.

African Americans living in Allegheny County in the 1950s weren't welcomed at the county's South Park swimming pool on Corrigan Drive. Instead, they were forced to swim at a separate but unequal facility at the park. What was the name of the pool reserved for blacks?

Sully Pool. It closed in the mid 1970s. In 1964, the pool was renamed East Drive Pool.

What was the first school in the U.S. to offer a PhD in existential phenomenological psychology?

Duquesne University.

Where in the Pittsburgh area is the only place to grow wheat, barley, millet and sorghum on a regular basis? It is also the only place in Pennsylvania to grow sugar cane!

At the Rodef Shalom Biblical Botanical Garden, which is located at Fifth and Morewood Avenues in Pittsburgh's Shadyside area.

Biblical garden at Rodef Shalom. Courtesy of Congregation Rodef Shalom and photographer Burton Hirsch.

In the early 1900s, the city of Pittsburgh was affluent enough to have not one but two millionaires' rows. What are the present-day street locations of the rows?

A section of Fifth Avenue in the Shadyside section of Pittsburgh and along Ridge Avenue on the city's North Side, the site of a few of the Allegheny County Community College buildings.

In what Allegheny County municipality was the nation's first home with a nuclear bomb shelter built?

On Mowry Drive in Pleasant Hills Borough. A family still lives in the structure, but the bomb shelter has been converted to a powder room.

In the early 1960s, University of Pittsburgh Chancellor Edward Litchfield unveiled a much publicized, but never built, real estate project which came to be known as "a skyscraper on its side." What was to be included in the project and where was its proposed site?

Plans included offices, museums and a nuclear reactor to be built in Panther Hollow, a ravine running between the University of Pittsburgh and Carnegie Mellon University.

In what Allegheny County town did Andrew Carnegie build his first United States Steel Mill and after whom did he name the plant?

Carnegie's first plant was in Braddock, PA. He named the plant after Edgar Thomson. At the time, Thomson was the president of the Pennsylvania Railroad and his line hauled Carnegie's products.

LaRoche College in Allegheny County is named after whom?

Mother Marie LaRoche. She was the daughter of a baroness, but gave up her claim to French nobility to become Mother Superior of the Sisters of Divine Providence in 1851.

What was the first enclosed shopping mall in the Pittsburgh area and when did it open?

South Hills Village opened its doors in July 1965.

How many locales in Allegheny County are recognized as national landmarks by the United States Government?

There are eight: The Allegheny County Court House and Jail, Kennywood, Oakmont Country Club, Smithfield Street Bridge, the confluence of the Monongahela and Allegheny Rivers at the Ohio, the Neville House in Collier Township, the Meadowcroft Rockshelter in Washington County, and Chatham Village on Pittsburgh's Mount Washington.

What was the name of the amusement park on the Parkway West that was removed to allow the building of a road to the new Pittsburgh International Airport?

White Swan Amusement Park.

Every Pittsburgh area school child knows that Fort Pitt and Fort Duquesne were built at the Point of the Golden Triangle during the nation's colonial period. What are the names of the two additional forts that were also built at the Point around the same time?

Fort Prince George and Mercer's Fort. Both forts were built by British soldiers and colonists.

Traces of Fort Duquesne and remnants of Fort Pitt, both built around mid 18th century, still exist at Pittsburgh's Point. Which fort was bigger and by how much?

About 12 Fort Duquesnes could fit into Fort Pitt. Fort Pitt, shaped like an irregular pentagon, occupied 17 acres.

How many panes of glass are in the six building complex at PPG headquarters?

19,750.

What Golden Triangle skyscraper was the first office building in the world to have an aluminum exterior?

Alcoa, naturally. It was built between 1951 and 1953.

How many panels make up the Mellon Arena roof?

Eight. It was built to open or close in 2 1/2 minutes.

How high is the tower at the Allegheny County Court House?

It is 325 feet—taller than a football field.

Since it was built in 1882, how many times were inmates successful in tunneling out of the now-closed Western Penitentiary State Correctional Institution?

Only four. Every escapee was caught. The most famous digger was Alexander Berkman. Berkman shot Henry Frick in Frick's office in 1892 during the Homestead Steel strike. At the time, Berkman had served eight years out of a 22-year sentence for the Frick shooting.

Where are the most posh pay phones in Pittsburgh?

Check out the two aesthetically pleasing pay phone booths in the Frick Building on Grant Street in downtown Pittsburgh. The exquisitely designed, glass-enclosed booths come with ornamental bronze grillwork and seats. Each would make a pleasant mini-office.

What was so special about East Pittsburgh's Valley telephone exchange in 1953?

It was the first telephone exchange in America to offer long-distance calling nationwide.

Who said Pittsburgh was "Hell with the lid taken off"?

James Parton in 1868. Parton was the most popular and important biographer in the United States during the last half of the 19th century.

What famous popular magazine was first published in Pittsburgh?

DeWitt Wallace, founder of Reader's Digest, *wrote promotional copy for a brief time for Westinghouse Electric.* Reader's Digest *made its debut in February 1922.*

Cleveland has the Rock and Roll Hall of Fame and Museum, and Seattle has the Experience Music Project. What does the University of Pittsburgh Student Union have?

The International Academy of Jazz.

What is the name of the white, Hindu temple high on a hill overlooking the Parkway East in Penn Hills?

Sri Venkateswara Temple. It was built in 1976 and was named after a temple in Tirupati, India.

What was the first African American church established in Pittsburgh?

The Bethel African Methodist Episcopal Church started in 1808. After being at several Pittsburgh locations, the church has been at Webster Avenue in the city's Hill District since 1959.

Commenting on Pittsburgh's role in a massive building project, a well-known Pittsburgh-born author wrote, "the City of Pittsburgh where some fifty different mills, foundries, machine shops, and specialty fabricators were involved ... making rivets, bolts, nuts (in the millions), steel girders, steel plates, steel forms for the lock-walls, special collapsible tubes by which the main culverts were formed, steel roller bearings (18,794 steel roller bearings) for the stem valves and spillway gates. The building of the gates themselves had been entrusted to McClintic-Marshall, a Pittsburgh contracting firm that specialized in heavy steel bridge construction." Who is the author, and from what book is the quote?

David McCullough. Path Between the Seas: Creation of the Panama Canal 1870-1914.

Where did Mrs. Bob Hope (Delores) receive the comedian's proposal to marry him?

At the William Penn Hotel in Pittsburgh. Delores Reed was a vocalist in a band playing at the hotel.

What were "Fulton's Follies"?

That was the name given to the two piers which stand, alone and aloof, on both sides of the Monongahela River between the Smithfield Street Bridge and the Point. At one time, former District U.S. Congressman James Fulton owned the piers.

How many calculations per second can the computer at the Pittsburgh Supercomputing Center perform?

The newest computer, Big Ben (named after Ben Roethlisberger and Ben Franklin), a CrayXT3, can perform 10 trillion calculations per second. Big Ben works alongside Lemieux, which computes at a rate of 6 trillion calculations per second. Big Ben is the 43rd most powerful computer in the world.

How many chicks have been hatched by the peregrine falcons on a 37th floor ledge of the Gulf Tower in downtown Pittsburgh?

Since the falcons arrived on the ledge in 1991, 47 falcon chicks have hatched there. Another 12 falcons have been hatched on the upper floors of the Cathedral of Learning since 2002.

The U.S. Environmental Protection Agency publishes what it calls a national priorities list of contaminated areas. The list is called the Super Fund and it lists areas contaminated substantially with hazardous waste. How many Super Fund sites are in the Pittsburgh area?

Eight. Four are in Allegheny County and four in Butler County.

What is so historically significant about the Bost Building on 8th Avenue in Homestead?

It is where the steelworkers had their headquarters during the Homestead Steel strike of 1892. It's now open to the public as a museum and as headquarters for the Steel Industry Heritage Corporation.

How fast does an elevator in the USX Tower go from the Grant Street level to the 62nd story?

It takes 30 seconds. The elevator travels at 1,600 feet a minute.

What was the first apartment house to open in downtown Pittsburgh?

According to Stefan Lorant's Pittsburgh: The Story of an American City, *it was the Bigelow on (where else) Bigelow Boulevard, across from the USX Tower. It opened on February 24, 1952.*

How many people does the University of Pittsburgh Medical Center (UPMC) employ and how large is its revenue?

About 40,000 people with a budget of over $5 billion.

Approximately how many medical residents receive training at the University of Pittsburgh Medical Center in any given year?

Around 1,300 in over 80 medical specialties.

The University of Pittsburgh was founded in 1787 but did not graduate its first female students until when?

1898. Sisters Margaret Lydia and Stella Mathilda Stein received bachelor degrees.

Where exactly is Freedom Corner in Pittsburgh and what does it signify?

It is at the intersection of Centre Avenue and Crawford Street in the city's Hill District. It is ground zero for civil rights activity in Pittsburgh.

How often do the three chandeliers in the Omni William Penn lobby receive a cleaning?

Once a year. Detail-oriented hotel employees hand-clean the 1,000-plus hand-cut prisms on each chandelier. The hotel has had the chandeliers since the 1960s and they cost about $150,000 each. They came from Czechoslovakia.

What public facility was at the corner of Fifth and Grant Street in downtown before the Frick Building replaced it in 1902?

A water reservoir that stored one million gallons of drinking water for city residents.

A mint on the pillow? The Presidential Suite
courtesy of the Omni William Penn Hotel.

What does it cost to stay at the Omni William Penn Hotel's Presidential Suite?

$2,800. That is a night, not a week! The 2,800 square feet of luxury includes a full kitchenette, a wet bar, separate dining area, sitting room, a marble entry, two king bedrooms and one bedroom with two double beds. Finally, you get triple-sheeted beds and fresh flowers. Mints on the pillow are extra.

Older Pittsburghers may remember ten large murals on the first floor walls of the Kaufmann's department store downtown. They were painted by Boardman Robinson, who along with Thomas Hart Benton, was a founder of the American mural movement of the 1930s. Where are the murals now?

They were sold to the Colorado Springs Fine Arts Center, which is near Denver. The murals were about 7 feet by 13 feet and sold in the 1990s, but were removed from Kaufmann's in the 1950s.

What Pittsburgh church has the largest collection of relics in the world outside of the Vatican?

Saint Anthony's Chapel on Pittsburgh's North Side has over 5,000 relics, placed there by Father Suibertus Gottfried Mollinger who built the church in 1880. Relics are body parts, or some personal memorial of a saint, martyr or other sacred person.

The United States Green Building Council promotes the construction of environmentally sound buildings. The group awards new buildings with high green standards prestigious certificates for Leadership in Energy and Environmental Design. How many greater Pittsburgh buildings have LEED certification?

Ten. The two most prominent are the PNC Firstside Center and the David L. Lawrence Convention Center, the first certified green convention center in the world. Other buildings include: CCI Center (South Side), Coro Center of Civic Leadership (South Side), Pennsylvania Department of Environmental Protection (California, PA), Greater Pittsburgh Community Food Bank (Duquesne, PA), CMU's Henderson House, CMU's New House Residence Hall, KSBA Architects (Lawrenceville), and the U.S. Steel Research Technology Center (Munhall). Finally, the Pittsburgh area leads the country in the amount of square feet of LEED certified buildings: 2,238,210 (as of 2/05).

The old Jones and Laughlin Hot Metal Bridge connects Pittsburgh's Second Avenue with the new South Side Works. What did the bridge carry when it was first built and what is the other bridge alongside it?

The Hot Metal Bridge carried molten iron from J & L's Hazelwood plant on the north side of the Monongahela River to the South Side plant. The iron was converted to steel and taken back to Hazelwood for rolling into finished steel products. The original Hot Metal Bridge will be converted to pedestrian and bicycle use and will link rail-trails on both sides of the river. The bridge parallel to it that now carries vehicular traffic is the old, so-called "Mon-Con" Bridge, short for Monongahela Connector (it linked rail lines on either side of the river).

The last blast furnace that remained standing at Jones and Laughlin Steel's South Side plant was named Ann. At what age did Ann meet her demise?

Ann was built in 1899 and was demolished on June 15, 1983. She was 270 feet tall and was named after one of the daughters of the company's founder.

An 18th century structure is an unusual sight in a modern city. In what city park does an 18th century log house co-exist with the 21st century?

In Schenley Park where the Neill log house, built around 1790, sits near the fifth hole of the golf course. A fine point: A log house uses squared logs that fit together. A log cabin, on the other hand, uses round logs and is not built to last.

The so-called "Skinny Building" is at Forbes and Wood in downtown Pittsburgh. Exactly how "skinny" is it?

It is 5 feet, 2 inches wide. It is vying with a building in Vancouver, British Columbia for the title of the thinnest building in North America.

Which is bigger, the rink at PPG Place or the rink at New York City's Rockefeller Center?

Pittsburgh's rink beats New York's. The ice surface at PPG Place is 9,600 square feet. Rockefeller Center's is a postage stamp size 7,200 square feet.

Saint Nicholas Roman Catholic Church on the North Side's East Ohio Street has what distinction?

It is the first Croatian church in America and was established in 1894.

What is so significant about the Emmanuel Episcopal Church on the North Side that enabled it to be named a National Historic Landmark?

The church, built in 1885, was designed by Henry Hobson Richardson, who was probably 19th century America's most prominent architect. Richardson also designed the Allegheny County Courthouse and Jail.

There's the John G. Rangos Sr. Research Center at the Children's Hospital of Pittsburgh, the Rangos Omnimax Theatre at the Carnegie Science Center, and the Rangos School of Health Sciences at Duquesne University. Who is John Rangos?

A local philanthropist who cleaned up in the waste disposal business. He sold his company, Chambers Development, to a national company.

How did Duquesne University's A. J. Palumbo Center and Pitt's Petersen Events Center get their names?

Each was named after contributors who helped finance the building. A.(Anthony) J.(Joseph) Palumbo is a coal mining magnate from Saint Marys (Elk County). The "Pete" is named after two people: Gertrude and John Petersen, husband and wife. John was an executive at Erie Insurance.

At its beginning, Point Park University had a different name. What is the school's original name and when was its first year of operation?

The school's roots go back to 1933 as a proprietary school named the Business Training College. It became Point Park Junior College in 1960, Point Park College in 1966 and, finally, Point Park University in 1998.

The Kraus Campo roof garden at the Posner Center. Courtesy of Carnegie Mellon University.

Where is the garden above located?

It's on the roof of Carnegie Mellon University's Posner Center. "Campo" is an Italian word for a central gathering place; the garden is named after its donors, CMU graduates Jill Gansman Kraus and her husband, Peter Kraus.

Three cylindrical dormitories on the University of Pittsburgh's Oakland campus are formally known as the Litchfield Towers, named after the ex-chancellor. Colloquially, however, they are known as what?

Ajax, Bab-O and Comet.

Where is the oldest wooden frame house in the city of Pittsburgh?

It is Chatham College's welcome center in Shadyside. The center was formerly the gatehouse of the estate of General Thomas Howe, a founder of the Republican Party. The house was built around 1860 and Chatham spent $2.2 million to restore it in 2003.

How much exhibit space does the new David L. Lawrence Convention Center have as compared to the old Lawrence Center?

About 2.5 times more exhibit space. The figures are 330,000 square feet versus 130,000 square feet. For comparison, McCormick Place, the largest convention center in the U.S., has 2.7 million square feet.

At the David L. Lawrence Convention Center, some of the walls talk . . . and sing and dance. How can that be?

That is because the Convention Center has three permanent venues displaying films of various Pittsburgh scenes on its walls. The screens are 40 feet by 5 feet, 17 feet by 5 feet, and 25 feet by 14 feet. It takes 17 computers, 18 projectors and over six miles of fiber optic cable to run the shows. They feature area people, artists, organizations, architecture and landscape. The shows last between six and 10 minutes.

For his design of the David L. Lawrence Convention Center and its swooping roof, New York architect Rafael Viñoly drew his inspiration from what distinctive Pittsburgh features?

The sloping lines of the Roberto Clemente, Andy Warhol and Rachel Carson bridges on the Allegheny River across from the Center.

The Lewis and Clark Expedition (1803-6) ended overlooking the Pacific Ocean in present-day Oregon. Where did the trek begin?

On August 31, 1803 Meriwether Lewis left from present-day Elizabeth Borough on the Monongahela River where he had the expedition's first boat made. Unfortunately, Lewis's boat builder was guilty of "unpardonable negligence" (he drank too much) and Lewis was delayed a bit before he went to meet up with Clark in Saint Louis. Lewis never did get around to firing the boat builder.

Media and Advertising

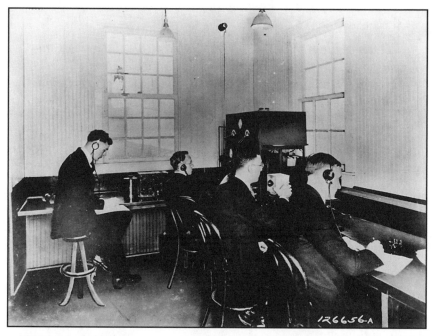

KDKA aired the first commercial radio broadcast from Pittsburgh. Seated left to right: R. S. McClelland, standby; William Thomas, transmitter operator; Leo H. Rosenberg, announcer; and John Frazier, telephone line operator. Courtesy of NewsTalk 1020 KDKA, Pittsburgh, Pennsylvania/CBS Radio.

PEOPLE AND PERSONALITIES

Who was "Your Platter Pushing Poppa," "Your Daddio of the Radio" and "Pork the Torque"?

> *WAMO's Porky Chedwick. Porky was born George Jacob Chedwick; he thanks his mother for "Porky." He went on air on August 1, 1948 on station WHOD, later changed to WAMO.*

For how long of a period was John Cigna the host of KDKA Radio's morning drive-time show?

> *18 years, from 1983 until 2001. He signed off on December 20, 2001.*

The former wife of a one-time New York City mayor was co-host of KDKA-TV's popular *Evening Magazine* when it first aired. Who is she?

Donna Hanover. The show first aired in the late 1970s and was on for 13 years. The original hosts were Hanover and Dave Durian. Donna was married to ex-New York mayor Rudy Guliani.

Which ex-Pittsburgh television anchor (KDKA-TV) once worked as an FBI agent?

Ray Tannehill.

Who was the host of WTAE-TV's *Bowling for Dollars*?

Nick Perry. The show went on the air in the 1960s and for a time it attracted more viewers than network newscasts did in the same time slot.

What were the names of Hank Stohl's puppet partners?

Rodney and Knish.

Who was the first person to appear in the *Pittsburgh Post-Gazette's* weekly "Dossier" feature?

Ex-WTAE-TV newscaster Don Cannon. The first dossier appeared in the February 25, 1984 edition. Cannon now does the news at KDKA-TV.

What was the name of Ricki's dog?

Copper. The show was, simply, Ricki and Copper. *The host was Ricki Wertz, and it aired on WTAE-TV from 1959-69. Copper died in 1967 and was replaced by Copper Penny.*

Which local television host served in the reign of Nosmo King?

Paul Shannon in his Adventure Time *television show on WTAE-TV.*

Hugo Black was nominated to the U.S. Supreme Court in 1937 by President Franklin Delano Roosevelt. What *Pittsburgh Post-Gazette* reporter won a Pulitzer Prize by uncovering Black's membership in the Klu Klux Klan in the 1920s, shortly after Black went on the court?

Ray Sprigle. Sprigle won the Pulitzer Prize in 1938.

Who was the first African American TV network news correspondent?

Pittsburgher Mal Goode. Goode was the grandson of slaves. He went to work for ABC in 1962 and died in 1995.

Which Pittsburgh television news anchor not only has an advanced degree in Asian studies, but also speaks a smattering of Japanese and Chinese?

WTAE's Sally Wiggin. Her Chinese name is Wei Shao-Li.

Wei Shao-Li (a/k/a Sally Wiggin). Courtesy of WTAE-TV.

What is the real name of the woman known as the "Shop 'n Save lady", that is, the woman who does commercials on television for Shop 'n Save?

Kathy Svilar.

Who was on the cover of the *Pittsburgh Magazine* edition that sold the most issues ever?

The December 1978 edition with Pittsburgh radio personality Jack Bogut on the cover sold 11,424 newsstand copies and had a total circulation of 56,580.

Which Pittsburgh area radio disc jockey has been on the air the longest?

Michael Komichak, the host of The Ukrainian Radio Program *on WPIT-AM (730) celebrated his 50th anniversary on the air in the year 2000. He is still on the air!*

Over his 48-year career, Paul Long established his reputation as a solid newsman while working at KDKA-TV and Radio and WTAE-TV. What *sport* did he broadcast and who was his partner?

Long did Pirates' games with Bob Prince in the 1950s.

Who hosted *Dance Party* on KDKA-TV in the late '50s and '60s?

Clark Race. The show was Pittsburgh's answer to Dick Clark's American Bandstand. *Race also appeared on KDKA Radio until 1970.*

Who was the star of WQED-TV's *Children's Corner?*

Josie Carey. The show aired between 1954 and 1961.

*KDKA's Bill Burns.
Courtesy KDKA-TV.*

Who bid adieu to the viewers of his 11 p.m. newscast with "good night, good luck, and good news tomorrow"?

Former KDKA-TV anchor Bill Burns.

Which zany Pittsburgh radio host created characters by the names of Carman Monoxide, Beauregard J. Cornpone, Omicron (he was from Venus), Screamin' Mad McEldowney and Baldwin McMoney (the richest kid in town)?

Rege Cordic, who was on KDKA Radio in the 1950s and '60s. Cordic also drank Olde Frothing Slosh beer. The brew was "pale, stale ale" and its foam was on the bottom. Cordic died in 1999.

Georgette the Fudgemaker, Norman the Castle Keeper, Stephen the Castle Prankster and Terminal Stare all starred in a show broadcast on WIIC-TV (now WPXI-TV) on Saturday nights from 1963 to 1983. The show featured classic horror movies. What was the show's name and who was its host?

Chiller Theatre *was the show hosted by Bill (Chilly Billy) Cardille. In the show, Cardille also played the roles of Captain Bad, Maurice the Matchmaker and the Little Old Monster Maker. Cardille also hosted* Studio Wrestling *on the same station.*

What Pittsburgh musical duo wrote *Since I Don't Have You* and *This I Swear*?

The music was written by Jimmy Beaumont of the Skyliners. The words were written by Joe Rock, a South Side native. The songs came out in the late 1950s. Beaumont comes from the South Hills section of Pittsburgh.

ON AIR, PART I

What were the call letters of the area's first commercial television station and what channel was it?

It was Channel 3 and its call letters were WDTV. The station was part of the now defunct Dumont television network. WDTV went on the air on November 1, 1950 and moved to Channel 2 in November 1952.

There are only two Pittsburgh area radio stations whose call letters begin with "K": KQV and KDKA Radio. Why is that?

KQV and KDKA had those call letters before the Federal Communications Commission, in the mid 1930s, passed a regulation requiring all radio stations west of the Mississippi River to have call letters start with "K" and stations east of the Mississippi River to have call letters that start with "W".

Before Channel 11 became WPXI, what were its call letters?

WIIC. "The ones to watch."

The "Fun Loving Five" appeared on what Pittsburgh radio rock station?

The term was applied to the various disc jockeys who played music on KQV when the station had a top-40 format.

The world's first commercial radio station, KDKA, went on the air in 1920. What was the first program?

It broadcast the presidential election returns on November 2, 1920. The race was between Warren G. Harding and James M. Cox. Harding won in a landslide.

On what date did *Mister Rogers' Neighborhood* first broadcast nationally on PBS?

February 19, 1968.

What percentage of the homes in the Pittsburgh area have cable television?

78.5 percent. Another 12.6 percent view their television via an alternate delivery system, such as home satellite. Satellite use has doubled in the past few years.

What do the letters in radio station WAMO stand for?

"W" is for east of the Mississippi River; "A" is for Allegheny; "M" for Monongahela; and "O" for Ohio.

What was KDKA Radio's *Party Line* phone number?

EX-1-1038. The show was hosted by Ed and Wendy King, both with encyclopedic memories.

Local television stations fight constantly to attract the highest number of viewers, but which one has the highest transmission tower?

WPXI at 848 feet. The tower is near the station's studio on the upper North Side.

On what day was the Pennsylvania Lottery's daily number "fixed" on the WTAE-TV drawing? What was the number?

On April 24, 1980, the lottery machine was rigged so that 666 would appear. The total statewide payout that day (legal or otherwise) for 666 was $3,502,425. WTAE-TV personality, Nick Perry, and a state lottery official were convicted in the fix. Two WTAE-TV stagehands pleaded guilty to participating in the drawing. Two other men (not WTAE employees) also received fines and probation. The station was not implicated in the fraud.

A Pittsburgh tradition, the KDKA-TV fundraising telecast for Children's Hospital of Pittsburgh, broadcast each year in mid-December, started in what year?

1954.

On Air, Part II: The Voices of Sports

Art McKennan was the Pittsburgh Pirates' public address announcer from 1948 until 1987. How many baseball games did he see?

About 5,500.

How many hours was Myron Cope on the air with his WTAE-AM sports talk show?

A Pittsburgh Post-Gazette reporter estimated in 1994 that Cope spent about 7,500 hours on the air over his nearly 22-year career as a talk show host. Yoi! Cope retired entirely from broadcasting in 2005; who knows how many more hours he had accrued by then.

Which former NBC sportscaster and *Today Show* host was once a Pittsburgh Pirates catcher?

Joe Garagiola.

Which former Pittsburgh Pirates player became a New York Mets broadcaster?

Left fielder Ralph Kiner who played between 1946-53.

Over his 48-year career, Paul Long established his reputation as a solid newsman while working at KDKA-TV and Radio and WTAE-TV. What *sport* did he broadcast and who was his partner?

Long did Pirates' games with Bob Prince in the 1950s.

For how long of a period did Bob Prince (nicknamed "The Gunner") broadcast Pirates baseball games? What year was he fired?

Prince started as the number two man to Rosey Rowswell in 1948 and was fired by KDKA in 1975.

One of "The Gunner's" broadcast partners was nicknamed after an animal. What was the partner's real name and his nickname?

The "Gunner's" partner was the "Possum," Jim Woods.

Paul Long (right) and "The Gunner" Bob Prince broadcasting a Bucs game. Courtesy Holly Van Dine.

After the firing of Bob Prince in 1975, what broadcast team came in to replace Prince and Nellie King?

Lanny Frattare and Milo Hamilton.

How long has Lanny Frattare been a Pirates broadcaster?

Frattare started calling games in 1976.

In Print

How many Pulitzer Prizes have been awarded to Pittsburgh newspaper reporters and photographers?

Eight. They are: 1938, Ray Sprigle (Pittsburgh Post-Gazette/ Reporting); 1971, John Paul Filo (Tarentum, New Kensington Valley Daily News and Daily Dispatch/Photography); 1986, Andrew Schneider and Mary Pat Flaherty (Pittsburgh Press/ Specialized Reporting); 1986, Andrew Schneider and Matthew Prelis (Pittsburgh Press/Meritorious Public Service); 1992, John Kaplan (Pittsburgh Post-Gazette/Photography); 1998 Martha Rial (Pittsburgh Post-Gazette/Photography).

On what day did the *Pittsburgh Post-Gazette* publish its first edition?

July 29, 1786. It was then known as the Pittsburgh Gazette. *The paper was distributed around the Fort Pitt area.*

What was the name of the monthly magazine that competed against WQED's *Pittsburgh Magazine* between June 1977 and January 1981?

Pittsburgher Magazine.

Until 1960, Pittsburgh had three major daily newspapers. In addition to the *Pittsburgh Press* and the *Pittsburgh Post-Gazette*, what other daily newspaper was there?

The Pittsburgh Sun-Telegraph.

How many copies of the *Pittsburgh Post-Gazette* are sold during the week? What about Sundays?

The daily circulation (paid copies) of the Post-Gazette *is around 232,500. Sunday's circulation is about 393,042. The number of people who actually read the* Post-Gazette *is about 622,000 on weekdays and 917,000 on Sundays. The figures are from November 2005.*

What magazine has the most sales on area newsstands?

People Weekly. In Touch *is second. Both are personality-driven magazines.*

When did the *Pittsburgh Courier* begin publishing?

The Courier *had a run of 500 copies on January 15, 1910. The idea for the paper came from Edwin Nathaniel Harleston, a guard at an H. J. Heinz company food plant. Harleston used the publication to print his poetry. At one time, the* Courier *was considered the most influential African American newspaper in the United States. It is now known as the* New Pittsburgh Courier.

SLOGANS FOR SALE

What company in its advertising campaign asked, "Who can?" and what baseball Hall of Famer was the company's spokesman?

American Heating. Ex-Pirates third baseman Pie Traynor was the pitchman.

What company's hamburger made you "happy to be hungry"?

Winky's. In its advertising, Winky's also boasted there was no Winky's in Wilmerding. Winky's was in business between the mid 1960s and the mid 1980s.

What local jewelry store not only sponsored a weekly-televised amateur hour but also offered E-Z credit?

Wilkens Jewelry.

What was Fort Pitt Beer's slogan?

It was short and sweet: "Fort Pitt, That's It."

What company had the "perfect sleeper"?

Rest assured! It was Serta Mattress Company.

Which company had the slogan "Three rooms, three ninety-eight"?

Olbum's Furniture Company on Pittsburgh's North Side.

"Aw, dry up!" could be interpreted as an impertinent injunction or it could be the slogan for a Pittsburgh-based company that began in 1949. Name the company.

It's Mariani and Richards, the waterproofing company. The slogan first appeared in a television commercial in 1952.

People from the Past

Mary Cardwell Dawson struck a high note in Pittsburgh's musical history. Courtesy of the Carnegie Library of Pittsburgh.

Who was John A. Brashear and where is he buried?

Brashear, a Pittsburgher, had a worldwide reputation as an astronomer and maker of lenses, mirrors, spectrograph plates, and other astronomical apparatus. He died in 1920 and his ashes are in a crypt at the Allegheny Observatory in Pittsburgh's Riverview Park.

Among his many talents, Andy Warhol had an interest in music. Warhol was a producer/manager for what rock group?

The Velvet Underground.

Combat bravery shows its face in many ways. Take Jack for example. Jack served in the Civil War as part of the Niagara Volunteer Fire Co., which had its headquarters in Pittsburgh's Strip District. Jack and his fellow soldiers saw action in numerous campaigns. Once, Jack was captured and exchanged for a Confederate soldier. He was captured a second time, but managed to escape. He was also wounded. He had a tendency to search battlefields looking for wounded or dead soldiers from his outfit. In 1864, he disappeared and was lost to history. Jack's portrait hangs in the Soldier and Sailors National Military Museum and Memorial in Oakland. What is so distinctive about Jack?

He was a dog! A mixed breed dog.

Where and when did the worst coal mine disaster in Pennsylvania occur?

On December 19, 1907, 293 miners were killed in an explosion at the Darr Mine located in Rostraver Township in Westmoreland County. Forty-nine of the victims are in a mass grave in Westmoreland's Olive Branch Cemetery. They join an additional 22 victims who also are buried there. Many of the dead were Hungarian immigrants. Austro-Hungarian Emperor Franz-Joseph helped to fund the building of a monument to memorialize the victims at the cemetery.

General George C. Marshall was the U.S.'s highest-ranking military officer during World War II. Where was he born?

In Uniontown, Pennsylvania in 1880. In his career, Marshall was an aide to General Pershing during World War I; became a five-star general during World War II; served as secretary of state from 1947 to 1949 and was secretary of defense (1951 to 1952). He also won the Nobel Peace Prize in 1953 for his work in promoting post-war recovery in Europe under what came to be known as the Marshall Plan. Quite a guy!

What Native American tribes were historically the most populous in the Western Pennsylvania area?

The Shawnee, Seneca, and Delaware.

Franklin Phillips was born in McKeesport in 1874. He enlisted in the U.S. Army in 1895 and fought in a major war where he came down with malaria. He didn't like the medical treatment he received and decided to go home to his mother. Three months later he tried to re-enlist but the Army turned him down, calling him a traitor. In 1899, he joined the Marines as Harry Fisher. A year later he was killed and received the Medal of Honor under his assumed name. The Navy even named a cargo ship after him. His mother tried to get the medal given in his real name and the Army agreed to do so, but the Marines balked. She also contacted President Woodrow Wilson about the name change, unsuccessfully. In the 1980s a retired steelworker from McKeesport, Wes Slusher, took up the hero's cause. Slusher finally persuaded the Marines to put Phillips/Fisher's medal in his real name and in 1988 the corps had a graveside ceremony to make the name change. In what wars did Phillips serve and where is he buried?

Phillips got malaria in the Spanish American War and was killed in the Boxer Rebellion. He is buried in the McKeesport and Versailles Cemetery. The name of Harry Fisher also appears on a monument in San Francisco's National Cemetery honoring the seven marines killed in the Boxer Rebellion.

Re-naming the Medal of Honor for Franklin Phillips at McKeesport and Versailles cemetery. Courtesy of the author.

Andrew Carnegie and Henry Clay Frick, owners of the steel mill at Homestead, PA, hired Pinkerton detectives to settle an infamous labor dispute. What is the name of Western Pennsylvania's bloodiest labor riot and when was it?

The Homestead Strike occurred on July 6, 1892. A gun battle resulted in 13 deaths and the vilification of Frick that lasts to this day in many circles. (Carnegie got off a bit easier – he was at his digs in Scotland at the time.)

Who was Joe Magarac?

Magarac was a mythical eastern European, early 20th century industrial worker who symbolized the brawn and industriousness of the Pittsburgh area heavy manufacturing employee. There is a statue of Magarac in the United Steel Workers Building lobby at Five Gateway Center.

Which famous naturalist was born in Springdale, PA near Pittsburgh and led a successful fight to ban the insecticide, DDT?

Rachel Carson. Her book, Silent Spring, *highlighted the dangers of insecticides. Carson was a 1929 graduate of what is now Chatham College; she died in 1964.*

On what Pittsburgh North Side street was the famous writer, Gertrude Stein, born?

Gertrude Stein was born at 850 Beech Street in what is now the Allegheny West section of Pittsburgh's North Side. Shortly after she was born in 1874, her family left the area.

One can easily argue that this woman, born in Pittsburgh in 1893, was the foremost figure in U.S. modern dance. Who was she?

Martha Graham. Graham was a teacher, dancer and choreographer. She created close to 150 works, including solos and some large scale presentations.

Which of these nationally-known pianists was *not* born in Pittsburgh: Oscar Levant, Bryan Janis or Jose Iturbi?

Jose Iturbi.

The Pittsburgh Opera has outlasted the Pittsburgh-based National Negro Opera Company (NNOC). Who started the NNOC and when?

Mary Cardwell Dawson, who studied at the New England Conservatory, started the NNOC in 1941 in the Homewood section of Pittsburgh. The NNOC mounted productions in Washington, DC, New York, Chicago and Pittsburgh. It closed in 1962.

Which Bridgeville High School graduate was the only man to coach a college and professional football team in the same year?

Aldo "Buff" Donelli. He coached the Pittsburgh Steelers and the Duquesne University football squad at the same time. This happened in 1941. In addition, Donelli excelled at soccer, playing for the U.S. in the 1934 World Cup. Donelli, who died in 1994, was also elected to the United States Soccer Hall of Fame.

In the War of 1812, Captain James Lawrence was the commander of the American frigate *Chesapeake*. His dying words in a battle near Boston Harbor were: "Don't give up the ship." What is the connection between Pittsburgh and Captain Lawrence?

The Pittsburgh neighborhood, Lawrenceville, is named in honor of Commander Lawrence.

Which University of Pittsburgh chemistry professor was the first person to isolate, identify and synthesize vitamin C?

Dr. Charles Glen King, in 1932. King spent five years on the project. With King's synthesizing of vitamin C, we were able to fight the ancient disease scurvy.

In 1856, this young man was born in Cresson, near Johnstown, with a great deal of wanderlust, apparently. He eventually traveled north, way north, discovering the North Pole in 1909. Who was he?

Robert E. Peary.

This muckraker was a graduate of Allegheny College. Her 1904 exposé, *History of the Standard Oil Company*, was an outgrowth of her father's boom or bust times in Titusville, Pennsylvania. What's her name?

Ida Tarbell.

This McKeesport writer, born in 1890, began his professional career as a Pittsburgh reporter, but eventually made it to Broadway, collaborating with George S. Kaufman, among others. He won the Pulitzer Prize for Drama in 1930 for his play *Green Pastures*. Name him.

Marc Connelly.

He won two Pulitzer Prizes for Drama, one in 1932 for *Of Thee I Sing*, a musical comedy satire on politics; the other in 1937 for *You Can't Take It With You*. Not bad for a man born in Pittsburgh in 1889 and who, for a while, lived on Walnut Street in the city's Shadyside district. Who was he?

George S. Kaufman.

Although she spent much of her early life in Europe, she was born on Pittsburgh's North Side in 1844. She went on to become one of the world's foremost Impressionist painters, particularly influenced by Edgar Degas. Among other paintings, she is known for *Woman Admiring Child* and *The Bath*. Name her.

Mary Cassatt.

Princess Ileana, daughter of King Ferdinand and Queen Marie, left her European home in 1948 after a communist take-over and eventually ended up in Ellwood City (Lawrence County) as Mother Alexandra, the founder of the Eastern Orthodox Monastery of the Transfiguration. Princess Ileana/Mother Alexandra is from what country?

Romania. She was born in 1906, became a U.S. citizen in the 1950s, took her vows in 1967, and soon started the Ellwood City monastery. Mother Alexandra chose Ellwood City because it reminded her of Romania. She died in 1991 and is buried at the monastery accompanied by a box of Romanian soil.

The Pirates could have used this Ellwood City-born slugger. In 1930, he drove in 191 runs as a Chicago Cub. His single season record still stands. He is?

Hack Wilson.

This religious leader, a convert to Catholicism, was known as the "Apostle of the Alleghenies." He was one of the first Roman Catholic priests to serve as a missionary to United States immigrants from Europe. He died in Loretto, PA in 1840. What's his name?

Demetrius Augustine Gallitzin. Gallitzin did a good job. At the time of his death, about 10,000 Roman Catholics lived in Western Pennsylvania. Four decades earlier, there were only 12.

He was born in Geneva, Switzerland, but settled near Uniontown. In 1801, he became the second U.S. secretary of the treasury, succeeding Alexander Hamilton. He also was elected to the U.S. House of Representatives in 1795. He eventually found time to serve as minister to France and Great Britain. Many Western Pennsylvanians learned to "bank" on his name. Who was he?

Albert Gallatin.

In 1867, he became a professor of physics and astronomy at the University of Pittsburgh. In 1896, he was the first person to build a successful, unmanned airplane. His craft, propelled by a steam engine, flew 4,200 feet over the Potomac River. If he had not had difficulties with a launch catapult nine days before the Wright Brothers flight at Kitty Hawk, some aviation historians believe he would have been the first person to fly an airplane. Who was he?

Samuel P. Langley.

By what other names is the U.S. Army's 99th Infantry Division known? During December, 1944, in what famous World War II battle did the 99th fight?

The 99th Infantry Division was established in 1921 as the "Pittsburgh Division". It also became known as the "Checkerboard Division" because its symbol was the coat of arms of William Pitt featured in checkerboard design. The 99th fought in the Battle of the Bulge.

Which Pittsburgher, born in Croatia in 1903 as Stejepan Mesaros, became the head of the Communist party in Western Pennsylvania in the 1950s and studied at the Lenin Institute in Moscow? (He was also convicted under state and federal laws for his political activity, but those convictions were overturned by the U.S. Supreme Court in 1956 in a significant free speech decision.)

Steve Nelson.

Who is the Reverend John Laboon?

Rev. John Laboon was a 1939 graduate of Central Catholic High School in Pittsburgh. He served in the submarine service during World War II, receiving the Silver Star for combat bravery. He eventually became a navy chaplain and served in Vietnam as a battlefield chaplain with a marine division. In Vietnam, he was awarded the Legion of Merit. In 1995, the United States Navy commissioned a new destroyer, the USS Laboon. *Laboon died in 1988.*

She was born Elda Furry, the daughter of a butcher, in Hollidaysburg, near Altoona. Who was she known as in Hollywood?

As Hedda Hopper, Furry became infamous as a prominent gossip columnist. She was a vicious competitor of Louella Parsons. The two of them controlled much of Hollywood publicity in the 1940s and 1950s.

Which Pittsburgher served as U.S. secretary of the treasury under three different presidents?

Andrew W. Mellon. He served under presidents Harding, Coolidge and Hoover.

The founder of the Boy Scouts of America was born in what is now Plum Borough (Allegheny County) in 1858. What is this "trustworthy, loyal, helpful, friendly, etc." man's name? (Hint: A county park is named after him.)

W. D. Boyce.

In August, 1859, Colonel Edwin Drake tapped the first subterranean supply of petroleum near Titusville, Crawford County. Considering the personal fortunes made in the oil business since then, did Drake leave an estate worth more than a million dollars or less than a million when he died in 1880?

A lot less than a million dollars. Drake spent some of his later life existing on a state government check.

Throughout the entire span of United States history, how many military service people from Allegheny County have won the U.S. Medal of Honor?

59.

Which World War II hero and Korean War commanding general (he replaced General Douglas MacArthur), spent most of his retirement years living in Fox Chapel?

General Matthew B. Ridgway. He moved to Pittsburgh to become chairman of the board of trustees of the Mellon Institute for Industrial Research. He died in 1993.

Which ex-Stowe Township resident is buried very near the John F. Kennedy grave site at Arlington National Cemetery?

Former Pennsylvania Supreme Court Justice, Michael A. Musmanno. Prior to becoming a Supreme Court justice, Musmanno served on the Allegheny Court of Common Pleas. He served on the State Supreme Court from 1952 until 1968. Musmanno qualified for burial in Arlington because he was a Lieutenant Commander in the U.S. Naval Reserve, and in World War II, he was appointed military governor in southern Italy after the Allies occupied Italy.

Richard Thornburgh, former governor of Pennsylvania, went on to serve as the attorney general of the United States. Which other Pittsburghers served in that position?

Brownsville lawyer Philander Chase Knox was attorney general between 1901 and 1904 and George Woodwark Wickersham served from 1909 to 1913. Wickersham practiced law in Pittsburgh.

Who is known as Pittsburgh's "Father of the Parks," especially for his efforts in establishing Highland and Schenley parks in the City of Pittsburgh?

Edward M. Bigelow, who was Pittsburgh's Director of Public Works. In 1889, it was Bigelow who persuaded Mary Schenley, who was living in England, to donate her farmland for a park in Oakland.

Which Pittsburgh-based evangelist from the 1940s to the 1970s, appeared on radio and television throughout the world and became what many consider to be the most famous woman evangelist of the 20th century?

Kathryn Kuhlman. Among other places, Kuhlman appeared at the old Carnegie Auditorium on Pittsburgh's North Side. She also appeared at the First Presbyterian Church downtown.

Who was the dissident United Mine Workers Union member who, along with his wife and daughter, was murdered at the bidding of then-UMW President Tony Boyle?

Joseph "Jock" Yablonski. The murders took place on December 31, 1969 at the victims' home in Washington County.

How many Pittsburghers have served on the United States Supreme Court?

Two. George Shiras Jr. was appointed to the Court in 1892 by Benjamin Harrison. He served until 1903 and died in 1924; he is buried in Allegheny Cemetery in Pittsburgh. The other was Henry Baldwin, who practiced law in Pittsburgh. Baldwin served on the court, 1830 to 1844. He was nominated by Andrew Jackson.

Which U. S. President briefly attended Allegheny College in Meadville, PA?

William McKinley.

Who was Pittsburgh's first artificial heart recipient?

Thomas Gaidosh, on October 24, 1985. Dr. Bartley Griffith implanted a Jarvik into Gaidosh, who died of cancer in 1996.

Who was John Daniel Norment?

The first European baby born in what is now Pittsburgh. He was born on September 18, 1755.

Who is considered to be the "father of daylight savings time" in the United States?

Robert Garland. Garland served on Pittsburgh's City Council from 1911 to 1939. He was also president of Pittsburgh's Chamber of Commerce. The U.S. Congress originally passed a daylight-savings bill in 1918, but repealed it in 1919. It was not until 1966 that Congress finally passed the Uniform Time Act setting up the present system.

When Pittsburgh-born composer Stephen Collins Foster died in 1864, how much of a fortune did he leave?

He died broke. Foster was born in the Lawrenceville section of Pittsburgh in 1826. He sold the rights to Oh, Susanna *for $100. In 1857, he sold all rights to future songs for about $1,900. The composer of* Camptown Races, My Old Kentucky Home, Old Dog Tray, Beautiful Dreamer *and* Jeannie with the Light Brown Hair *spent most of his life in debt. The profits from his songs went largely to performers and publishers. He became an alcoholic and died nearly penniless.*

Phipps Conservatory is constructed primarily with glass, although the conservatory's benefactor made his fortune in iron and steel. What Pittsburgher presented the conservatory to the city?

Henry Phipps, who was a partner of Andrew Carnegie in the Carnegie Company, which became U.S. Steel. The conservatory opened on December 7, 1893. Phipps was born in 1839, the son of an immigrant cobbler. He also built the Fulton Building on Sixth Street downtown, now site of the Renaissance Pittsburgh Hotel. Phipps, who died in 1930, named the Fulton Building after Robert Fulton, the steamboat inventor.

Henry Ossawa Tanner made history at the White House. Courtesy of the Carnegie Library of Pittsburgh.

Henry Ossawa Tanner, 1859-1937
America's First Major Black Painter

Artist Henry Ossawa Tanner was born in Pittsburgh in 1859 and was considered by many to be the best African American artist of his day. How is he part of White House history?

One of Tanner's paintings, Sand Dunes at Sunset, Atlantic City, *is the first painting by an African American artist to become part of the White House permanent art collection. The painting entered the collection on October 29, 1996.*

The character of Nick Charles in six *Thin Man* films was played by what actor born in Pittsburgh in 1892?

William Powell. Powell received three Academy Award nominations in his career. Together, he and Myrna Loy appeared in 14 films. Powell died in 1984.

A Pittsburgh native, Alfred Cleveland, wrote the lyrics. Marvin Gaye recorded the song. Among other things, the lyrics said, "war is not the answer." What is the song?

What's Going On.

On July 17, 1938, a 31-year old pilot took off from Brooklyn, NY for Long Beach, CA. Twenty-eight hours and 13 minutes later he landed. In Dublin, Ireland. His lapse in finding his way made him an international hero. In fact, Allegheny County named a road in South Park after him. Who was the "wrong-way" aviator?

Douglas "Wrong-way" Corrigan. Corrigan was born in 1907 in Galveston, TX and he probably didn't make a navigational error. Evidently, the federal government wouldn't let him fly his airplane, a 1929 Curtis-Robin monoplane, across the Atlantic so he filed a flight plan for California and headed east instead of west upon take-off. He returned to New York by steamship to a ticker-tape parade with more than a million people lining the street, a turnout larger than Charles Lindbergh's following his transatlantic flight. Allegheny County named South Park's Corrigan Drive after him. The road was previously called Cat Fish Run Road. Corrigan died in 1995.

Why did Pittsburgher Harry K. Thaw kill Stanford White in 1906?

Stanford White was one of America's best-known architects. He also liked young girls. Evelyn Nesbit, a showgirl, was one of White's conquests when she was 16. Thaw married Nesbit, but could not cope with the fact that White took his wife's virtue. Thaw shot White in the Madison Square Garden in New York. Thaw was heir to a Pittsburgh coal and railroad fortune.

In 1922, Mrs. Minnie Penfield had the distinction of being the first woman to do what in Allegheny County?

On January 9, 1922, Mrs. Penfield became the first woman to serve on a jury.

Which Allegheny County district attorney committed suicide hours before he was indicted by a federal grand jury for income tax fraud on March 5, 1974?

Robert W. Duggan.

Before he became a best-selling author and an anti-war activist, what did Dr. Benjamin Spock do in Pittsburgh?

In 1953, he helped found the Arsenal Family and Children's Center. The Center was started by the University of Pittsburgh Department of Education, but is now a private nonprofit group. The center specializes in child development.

Who was Calbraith Perry Rodgers?

Pittsburgh-born Rodgers was the first person to fly across the United States. He started from Long Island, New York on September 17, 1911 and landed in Long Beach, California on November 5, 1911. He was in the air for 82 hours and 4 minutes. Rodgers was born in Pittsburgh in 1874 and died in Long Beach in 1912.

Which Roman Catholic Church saints lived together at the same time at the same church in Pittsburgh?

In the mid 1800s, future saints Francis Seelos and John Neumann, before becoming saints, served at the Saint Patrick parish on Liberty Avenue in Pittsburgh's Strip District.

Only one ocean liner has had Pittsburgh in its name. When did the USS *Pittsburgh* first sail?

The USS Pittsburgh *started her maiden voyage June 6, 1922 traveling from Liverpool to Boston. In 1926, her name was changed to* Pennland II. *In April, 1941, she was sunk by German bombers.*

April 10, 1845 was a big news day in Pittsburgh. What happened?

A fire covering 24 blocks on 56 acres swept through downtown. Almost 1,200 buildings were destroyed, about 1/3 of the city. The estimated loss was $9 million.

When, in all likelihood, was the last time a member of the Ku Klux Klan was shot and killed in the Pittsburgh area?

August 26, 1923. A day after a Klan initiation in Scott Township attended by 20,000 members, the Klan paraded in Carnegie. A riot broke out and a Klansman from Washington County was killed. A Carnegie undertaker was arrested for the shooting. Pennsylvania Klan leaders offered $5,000 in rewards: $2,500 for information leading to more arrests and/or convictions for the killing; $2,500 for the arrests and/or convictions of those who started the riot.

Why would the alumni and friends of Saint Vincent College genuflect at the mention of Boniface Wimmer?

Because he founded the school in 1846. Wimmer was born in Bavaria in 1809 and came to America in 1846. At one time, he was the head of the Benedictine Order in America. He died in 1887.

The worst Civil War disaster for the north occurred in Pittsburgh on September 17, 1862. What happened and how bad was it?

A plant where cartridges were loaded and gun parts were manufactured exploded. Seventy-eight workers died, most of them young women or teenage girls. Today, the Arsenal Park ballfield in Lawrenceville is at the explosion site.

Where can a Civil War buff find a listing (alphabetical, no less) of Allegheny County residents who served in that war? By the way, how many did serve?

The Western Pennsylvania Genealogical Society in Oakland has the list in a book it has published: Allegheny County in the War For the Suppression of the Rebellion 1861 to 1865. *25,930 served.*

In 1909, William Howard Taft was the first sitting U.S. president to visit a synagogue. Which one did he visit?

The Rodef Shalom Congregation at Fifth and Morewood in Oakland.

In 1990 the Pennsylvania Crime Commission called Pittsburgh's Tony Grosso "Pennsylvania's undisputed illegal lottery kingpin." How much money did the commission estimate Grosso grossed annually?

More than $30 million each year. He had anywhere from 3,000 to 5,000 bookies working for him. Grosso went to prison in 1986.

Edgar J. Kaufmann, the former head of Kaufmann's Department Store and the builder of Fallingwater, was unorthodox in his choice of homes, artwork and personal relationships. For a perfect example: Where was his wife laid out when she died in 1952?

On a chaise-lounge in the Kaufmanns' apartment in the William Penn Hotel. In 1954, at age 68, Kaufmann married his stenographer/nurse/companion. She was 34.

Who is considered the "father" of C.P.R. (cardio-pulmonary resuscitation)?

The University of Pittsburgh's Dr. Peter Safar, who died in 2003. Safar started the International Resuscitation Research Center at Pitt in 1979. He was an anesthesiologist.

Hugh J. Ward hit the jackpot when he originated this game in Pittsburgh during the early 1920s. What was the game?

Bingo. He ran the game at local carnivals, but went national in 1924. He received a bingo copyright in 1933.

"One Shot" was the nickname given to which Pittsburgh photographer? What did the phrase signify? Who gave it to him?

Mayor David L. Lawrence gave the handle to Charles "Teenie" Harris, a photographer for the Pittsburgh Courier. *"One Shot" referred to Harris's ability to capture a scene while other photographers were still fumbling with their lenses. He learned to do this out of necessity because his budget for film was small.*

Harris was born in Pittsburgh's Hill District in 1928 and died in 1998. He supposedly agreed to give the rights to his photos to a local businessman who, in turn, would pay Harris royalties. Harris received neither the royalties nor the return of his collection. In 1998, Harris sued to get his photos back. In 2000, his family received the photos after a three-week trial.

In his 42-year career as a photographer for the *Pittsburgh Courier* newspaper, Charles "Teenie" Harris took thousands of photos, primarily of scenes in Pittsburgh's African American community. What Pittsburgh institution now has about 80,000 negatives of Harris' in its archives?

The Carnegie Museum of Art bought the 80,000 negatives in 2001.

Which short-term resident of Pittsburgh became the U.S.'s first African American woman millionaire?

That distinction belongs to Madam C. J. Walker, who made her fortune in the hair treatment/cosmetic business. Walker was born in 1867 as Sarah Breedlove to freed slaves in Louisiana. She married a newspaperman, Charles James Walker, in 1906 and moved to Pittsburgh in 1907 or 1908 because Pittsburgh's rail lines enabled her to ship her products more efficiently. She had a shop in Pittsburgh's Hill District and lived in Shadyside. She and her fortune ended up in New York City. She also had an estate in Westchester County near the Rockefeller estate; it is now a National Historic Landmark.

Nellie Bly made Phileus Fogg look like a slowpoke. Courtesy Carnegie Library of Pittsburgh.

Phileus Fogg, Jules Verne's character from *Around the World in Eighty Days* (1873), was a slacker compared to an investigative journalist born in Apollo, PA. In 1889-90 she traveled the world in 72 days, 6 hours, 11 minutes and 14 seconds. Who was she?

Nellie Bly. Bly was born in Apollo in May, 1864. Her trip gave her worldwide fame. She started her newspaper career in Pittsburgh in 1885 and she died in 1922. She was born Elizabeth Cochran, but a newspaper editor suggested she take a pen name from a Stephen Foster song. The newspaper sponsoring her trip, The New York World, *collected close to one million entries from readers trying to guess Bly's time.*

Why should local bibliophiles offer thanks to William Bently, William M. Darlington, Rachel McMasters Miller Hunt, Charles Rosenbloom and James Winthrop?

Each donated major book collections to local academic libraries: Darlington to the University of Pittsburgh, Hunt and Rosenbloom to Carnegie Mellon University, Bently and Winthrop to Allegheny College. The early 19th century contributions by Bently and Winthrop made Allegheny College's library one of the finest in the country (the college opened in 1823).

How many military service people from Allegheny County died while serving in the Vietnam War?

408.

This author came to Pittsburgh in 1895 to become the managing editor of a new family magazine, *The Home Monthly*. She lived for a while on Murray Hill in Shadyside. Eventually, she became the editor of *McClure's*, a muckraking monthly periodical. Her novels include: *Alexander's Bridge* (her first), *O Pioneers!*, *My Antonia*, *One of Ours* (a Pulitzer Prize winner), and *A Lost Lady*. Her name is?

Willa Cather.

This woman, born in the Beechview section of Pittsburgh in 1919, became a polarizing figure in the 1950s and 1960s because of her atheistic views. Referred to as the "most hated woman in America," she founded American Atheists, a national group that worked for the civil rights of nonbelievers and for the separation of church and state. What is her name?

Madalyn Murray O'Hair. O'Hair disappeared in 1995. Her burned and dismembered body was found in 2001. One of her employees pleaded guilty to the murder of O'Hair and her two children.

Which Pittsburgh heiress was the inspiration for the Irving Berlin musical, *Call Me Madame*?

Perle Mesta, wife of George Mesta, the founder of Mesta Machine in West Homestead (the company made machinery for the steel industry). She inherited George's fortune when he died in 1925 and spent much of her life leading a highly social life. She became an ambassador to Luxembourg (that's where Call Me Madame *comes in). Lyndon and Lady Bird Johnson bought her Washington, DC house. She died in 1975 and is buried in Pittsburgh's Homewood Cemetery next to her husband.*

Joan Mrlik was born in November 1928, but her mother abandoned her by Christmas Eve. Joan was left at a theater in East Liberty where the theater manager and a still unknown Gene Kelly found her. Kelly and 10 other members of a club he belonged to adopted Joan. What is the club's name?

Back then it was the Variety Club. Today, Variety Clubs International raises money for disadvantaged children. Variety has 50 active chapters in the U.S. and chapters in 13 foreign countries. Joan became a registered nurse and served in the navy during the Korean War. She died in 1994.

Civil engineer Mao Yisheng helped design the Great Hall of the People in Beijing, China. He was also the chief engineer for the first Yangtze River Bridge at Wuhan. What "first" did Mao achieve in Pittsburgh in 1919?

He was the first person to receive a PhD from Carnegie Institute of Technology (now Carnegie Mellon University). Mao died in 1993 at age 93. His PhD was in engineering.

Mao Yisheng, a Pittsburgh "first." Courtesy Carnegie Mellon University.

Who is considered the "Father of Flag Day" (June 14)?

Collier Township (Allegheny County) resident William T. Kerr. Kerr spent almost his entire life campaigning to make Flag Day a national holiday. He started in 1882, but wasn't successful until 1949 when Kerr stood beside President Harry Truman while Truman signed the Flag Day bill into law.

An adventuresome person asking Pittsburgh Phil for advice would get practical tips covering what sport?

Horse racing. Phil was born as George E. Smith in Sewickley in the early 1860s. He was a handicapper as well as a bettor. Although he lived in Pittsburgh (actually Allegheny City, since annexed and known as the North Side), he spent much of his time at tracks throughout the country. He got his nickname in a Chicago poolroom from Silver Bill Riley who thought poolrooms were full of people named "Smith." Phil died in 1905 and is buried in the North Side's Union Dale Cemetery. He left an estate worth $1.7 million (that's about $35 million in today's dollars). On top of his $30,000 mausoleum, his mother placed his statue—holding a racing program.

Although he was a master of self-promotion through the black and white sandwich boards he hung around his neck, and even though he was well-known throughout the Pittsburgh area, he claims he could not receive his mail. Who was he?

Bob Lansberry. Lansberry claimed the CIA was behind a plot to stop his mail. He died in 1999.

LAY OF THE LAND

Pittsburgh under water during the 1936 Saint Patrick's Day Flood. Photo by Frank E. Bingaman from the Stefan Lorant Iconography Collection. Courtesy of the Carnegie Library of Pittsburgh.

How high did the water crest in the 1936 Saint Patrick's Day Pittsburgh flood?

At a record 46 feet.

What are the city of Pittsburgh's coordinates on a map?

40 degrees 26 minutes N, 80 degrees 0 minutes W.

What major city in Spain is on almost the same parallel as Pittsburgh?

Madrid.

What do Pittsburgh and Ecuador have in common?

Both are on the same longitude.

How many trees are growing on streets in the city of Pittsburgh?

A 2005 survey completed by Pittsburgh's Shade Tree Commission came up with 31,524. A 1995 survey undertaken by Carnegie Mellon University students had an estimate of 40,000 street trees.

Where is Allegheny County's oldest tree?

The oldest-known tree is a white ash on Parkside Avenue in Mount Lebanon. It has an estimated age of over 400 years. Some reports not only consider it the oldest tree growing in Allegheny County, but also the largest.

What is the largest man-made body of water in Allegheny County?

The lake at North Park covers about 75 acres.

A new animal species was found recently in the Allegheny River. What was the species?

Give a warm, wet welcome to the tiny zebra mussel.

If you travel downstream from the confluence of the Monongahela and Allegheny rivers, down the Ohio and the Mississippi, you will eventually reach New Orleans. How much lower is the elevation between New Orleans and the Golden Triangle?

Seven hundred and ten feet. New Orleans is at sea level. The Point is at about 710 feet.

On the downtown side of the Fort Pitt Tunnel, which portal is lower, the one coming into downtown or the one leaving downtown?

It is the one leaving downtown. The upper portal provides the magnificent view of the Golden Triangle as you enter Pittsburgh through the Fort Pitt Tunnel.

Allegheny County is how many square miles?

Allegheny County is 730.74 square miles. Within Allegheny County the four largest municipalities are: Pittsburgh (55.38 square miles), Findlay Township (32.42 square miles), Plum Borough (28.88 square miles), and West Deer Township (28.65 square miles).

How many miles of riverfront are in Allegheny County?

170 miles counting both sides of the river.

Geologically speaking, what is the Pittsburgh coal seam?

It is one of the largest single seams of coal in the world and is one of the world's most valuable, recoverable resources. In some places, the seam is 500 feet deep. It runs from Huntington, West Virginia to about 75 miles north of Pittsburgh. Its western border is about 125 miles from Pittsburgh and on the eastern side, it is in Cambria County.

How much park space/open space is within the city of Pittsburgh?

There are 2,735 acres of "green" space within the city. That's 7.7 percent of all the land in the city or 862 residents for every acre. San Diego has close to 18 percent of its land devoted to park space.

In size, how does New York's Central Park compare to Pittsburgh's Frick and Schenley parks?

Central Park is 840 acres. Combined, Frick and Schenley exceed the size of Central Park by nearly 75 acres. Frick has 456.8 acres, Schenley, 456 acres.

What is the highest point of elevation in Allegheny County?

There are two equally high points at 1400 feet: One is in Plum Borough, another is in South Park Township on the Allegheny/Washington County line.

What is the lowest point of elevation in the Pittsburgh area?

It is on the Ohio River in Beaver County where the borders of Pennsylvania, Ohio and West Virginia intersect. The elevation is 660 feet. The lowest point in Allegheny County (680 feet) is on the Ohio River at the Beaver County line.

What is the highest point of elevation in the six-county Pittsburgh area?

Laurel Hill in Springfield Township, Fayette County is 3,000 feet high. Another high point in Fayette County is at another section of Laurel Hill. A part of Laurel Hill in Salt Lick Township measures 2,940 feet.

What is the flood stage at the Point in downtown Pittsburgh?

It is 25 feet. The National Weather Service defines flood stage as the point at which significant flooding occurs. The parking lot on the Monongahela River near the Point gets minor flooding at 18 feet.

What two rivers meet at Fairmont, West Virginia to form the Monongahela River?

The West Fork and Tygart.

What is the date for "Rain Day" in Waynesburg and what is the likelihood of any rain falling in the Washington County town on that day?

The date is July 29 and over the last 30+ years there has been more than an 80 percent chance of rain in any given year.

What were the driest and wettest *months* on record in the Pittsburgh area?

Driest: October 1874, with 0.06 inches of precipitation.

Wettest: November 1985, with 11.05 inches of precipitation.

What were the driest and wettest *years* on record in the Pittsburgh area?

In 1930, there were only 22.65 inches of precipitation, making it the driest year.

The wettest year was 2004 with 57.43 inches of precipitation, thanks to Hurricanes Frances and Ivan.

On what day did the Pittsburgh area have its greatest daily rainfall?

September 17, 2004: 5.95 inches of rainfall due to remnants of Hurricane Ivan.

September 8, 2004: 3.60 inches due to remnants of Hurricane Frances.

Other heavy rain days: August 21, 1888: 3.57 inches.

October 15, 1954: 3.56 inches (Hurricane Hazel).

What is the *latest* it has ever snowed in the area?

There was a trace of snow on May 31, 1893 and one-half inch fell on May 25, 1925.

What is the *earliest* it has snowed in the Pittsburgh area?

There was a trace of snow as early as September 23, 1989 and 1.8 inches fell on October 18, 1972.

During what winter season did the most snow fall in Pittsburgh?

In 1950-51, the total snowfall was 82.0 inches. That is nearly twice the average annual snowfall.

"Zoogeography" is the study of the geographical distribution of animals and animal communities. In what zoogeographical region does the Pittsburgh area lay?

The Neartic region, specifically the Allegheny sub-region.

The borough of Charleroi in Washington County has the same name as a city in what European country?

Belgium.

Loyalhanna Creek in Westmoreland County joins with the Conemaugh River in Indiana County to form what river?

The Kiskiminetas River.

Where is the Ohio River at its most northern point?

At Rochester Borough in Beaver County.

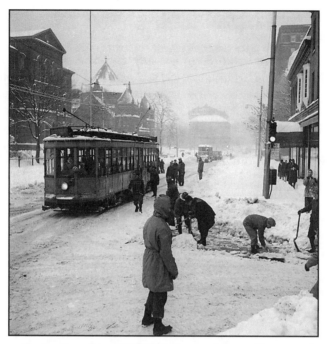

During the winter of 1950-51, the weather outside was truly frightful. This photo was taken in December, 1950. Courtesy Carnegie Library of Pittsburgh.

I f it is noon Greenwich Mean Time, what time is it in Pittsburgh?

7:00 a.m. There is a five-hour time difference for 51 weeks a year. Britain goes on British Summer Time one week before the U.S. goes on Daylight Savings Time.

H ow many days of sunshine does the Pittsburgh area average each year?

It is clear on an average of 58.3 days, partly cloudy 103.3 days and cloudy 203.6 days.

H ow windy is Pittsburgh?

The wind blows at an average 9.1 miles per hour.

What are the hottest and coldest temperatures ever recorded for the Pittsburgh area?

It hit 103 degrees three times: July 16, 1988, August 6, 1918 and July 10, 1881. January 19, 1994 was the coldest at a minus 22 degrees.

On average, how much snow falls in the Pittsburgh area each year?

43.8 inches.

On average, how much precipitation falls in the Pittsburgh area each year?

36.85 inches.

How far is Pittsburgh from these cities: Bombay, Buenos Aires, Calcutta, London, Los Angeles, Mexico City, Moscow, New York, Osaka, Paris, Rio de Janeiro, Sao Paulo, Seoul, and Tokyo?

City distances (miles) from Pittsburgh: Bombay, 7,987; Buenos Aires 5,323; Calcutta, 8,034; London, 3,725; Los Angeles, 2,145; Mexico City, 1,838; Moscow, 4,868; New York, 318; Osaka, 6,787; Paris, 3,898; Rio de Janeiro, 4,946; Seoul, 6,797; Tokyo, 6,619.

How far is Pittsburgh from the South Pole, the North Pole and the equator?

Pittsburgh is 9,004.5 miles from the South Pole; 3,415.5 miles from the North Pole; 2,835 miles from the equator.

How many of Allegheny County's smallest municipalities can fit snuggly into North Park?

The 85 smallest municipalities can be placed inside North Park with some room left for a putting green.

Which Allegheny County park is bigger: North Park or South Park?

North Park has 4.7 square miles of space. South Park is 3.1 square miles in size. By acreage, it's North Park: 2,729 acres; South Park: 2,188 acres.

Where does the Beaver River flow into the Ohio River?

Between Bridgewater and Rochester about 25.5 miles past the Point in Pittsburgh. The Beaver River is formed by the confluence of the Shenango and Mahoning rivers in Lawrence County.

What enormous body of water in Canada is on the same longitude as Pittsburgh?

Hudson Bay.

Pittsburgh isn't the only city famous for its three rivers. What German city, in Bavaria, is known as "the town of the three rivers"?

Passau is formed at the confluence of the Danube, Inn, and Ilz Rivers. Passau is about 111 miles northeast of Munich. A cathedral in Passau contains one of the largest church organs in the world, with 17,000 pipes.

At the equator, the circumference of the earth is about 25,000 miles. Since it takes the earth 24 hours to make a complete revolution, that means at the equator the earth is spinning just over 1,000 miles per hour. How fast is the earth spinning at Pittsburgh's latitude, which is about 40 degrees north of the equator?

Someone standing at Pittsburgh's latitude would be traveling about 766 miles per hour. Locations of latitude further away from the equator move slower than 1,000 mph to make a revolution. To figure out the speed of the earth's rotation at Pittsburgh's latitude take the cosine of 40 degrees X 1,000.

In terms of size, what is Allegheny County's smallest municipality?

Pennsbury Village is the smallest with 0.1 square miles of space. Four other municipalities are 0.2 square miles.

Here's a far out question—literally! What are *Brashear 5502, Carnegia 671, Caligiuri 42365* and *Misterrogers 26858*?

They are asteroids named after prominent Pittsburghers. Asteroids are rocky space objects that can be a few feet wide to several hundred miles wide. Most asteroids orbit in a belt between Mars and Jupiter and each has an assigned number.

What two local municipalities have asteroids named after them?

Pittsburgh and Allegheny. (Allegheny was a separate town annexed by Pittsburgh in 1907 and is now known as the North Side.) Astronomically speaking, the asteroids are Pittsburghia 484 *and* Alleghenia 457.

According to the book, *Extreme Weather,* by Christopher C. Burt, where is the wettest spot in Pennsylvania?

Burt says its Chalk Hill (Fayette County), which averages 54.04 inches of precipitation a year. Chalk Hill is a few miles southeast of Uniontown.

What is the coldest spot in Pennsylvania?

Christopher C. Burt in Extreme Weather *gives the ranking to Mount Pleasant in Westmoreland County. Historically, Mount Pleasant averages a daily minimum January temperature of only 9.9 degrees.*

GETTING FROM HERE TO THERE

No more free maps. No more cheap gas. Photo from the Gulf Oil Company, 1913. Courtesy of the Carnegie Library of Pittsburgh.

The city of Pittsburgh has lots of these, even more than Venice. What are they are and how many of them does Pittsburgh have?

Bridges. A 2005 count by Bob Regan, author of The Bridges of Pittsburgh, *shows 446 bridges within or at the city limits—that's more than Venice! And there are hundreds more in Allegheny County, although no one knows the exact number. In his 2005 book* The City of Falling Angels, *John Berendt (he also wrote* Midnight in the Garden of Good and Evil) *quotes Gianpietro Zucchetta, author of* Venice, Bridge by Bridge, *who claims Venice has 443 bridges; the Venice Bureau of Tourism gives the number as 400. Whatever the figure, Venice came up short against Pittsburgh.*

What is the *oldest* bridge in Pittsburgh?

The Second Avenue Bridge (in Hazelwood) over Nine Mile Run. The bridge existed as early as 1846. It is also the first all-steel bridge in America.

How many bridges are in Allegheny County?

There are about 1,058 bridges in Allegheny County that are at least 20 feet in length, although no one knows the exact number because of conflicting databases maintained by various government agencies. Whatever it is, it's a lot.

What is the area's longest bridge?

The Neville Island Bridge, measuring 4,544 feet long.

What was the name of the mass transit system the Allegheny County commissioners originally planned in the 1960s to run from South Hills Village to the Golden Triangle?

Skybus. Skybus was a rubber-wheeled, fully automated system that was to operate underground, at grade and in an elevated fashion. It was killed in the early 1970s because of extensive political opposition.

The bridge over the Allegheny River between Lawrenceville and Sharpsburg is the Fleming Bridge. In whose honor is the bridge named?

Robert D. Fleming. He was a prominent politician who spent 36 years in state government, ending his career as a state senator in 1974. He also served on the board of the Allegheny County Port Authority and was a strong proponent of the Skybus plan for mass transit.

Skybus: debated but never built. Photo by Paul Slantis, 1972. Courtesy of the Carnegie Library of Pittsburgh.

The Birmingham Bridge, which connects Pittsburgh's South Side with Oakland, replaced the nearby Brady Street Bridge that was demolished May 23, 1978. What horrible accident occurred during the demolition?

Two steel beams trapped the leg of an ironworker demolishing the Brady Street Bridge. A doctor amputated the man's leg while still on the bridge.

What is the area's longest tunnel?

The Liberty Tunnels, measuring 5,920 feet.

When did the Squirrel Hill Tunnels open?

June 5, 1953.

What was the *Flying Fraction*?

The Pittsburgh Railways Company, absorbed by the Allegheny County Port Authority, had a trolley with 77/54 as its destination. PAT's present day 54C bus travels over the same route as the old 77/54 trolley. The route goes from Carrick, through the South Side, Oakland, Bloomfield, the Strip District, the North Side and back.

What is so unusual about the neon lights at the Allegheny County Port Authority's "T" Steel Plaza stop (platform level)?

"Warm" neon lights glow in the morning, while in the evening "cool" neon colors predominate. They are part of a light sculpture designed by artist Jane Haskell.

Which nationally-known artist designed the mural at Port Authority's "T" Gateway Center subway stop?

Romare Bearden.

Hundreds of thousands of people have ridden Pittsburgh's Monongahela and Duquesne Heights inclines since they were built in the late 19th century without knowing who designed and built them. Who did?

Samuel Diescher, who was considered the country's foremost incline builder.

In 1992, the Allegheny County Port Authority bus and trolley operators went on strike. How long did the strike last? Was the 1992 strike the longest?

At twenty-eight days, the March-April 1992 strike was by far the longest; the next longest lasted only a few days.

On an average weekday, how many vehicles travel through the Fort Pitt Tunnels?

Close to 110,000. It is the area's most heavily-traveled spot.

What is the Port Authority's most heavily-used route?

The 61C McKeesport/Homestead, which hauls 9,104 passengers on an average weekday.

How many light rail vehicles and buses are in the Port Authority's fleet?

PAT has 83 light rail vehicles and 1,017 buses. There are also four incline plane cars.

How many Park and Ride lots does the Port Authority operate and how many parking spaces are in those lots?

There are 63 lots with 13,532 spaces. The largest is the South Hills Village lot with 2,732 parking spaces, including 2,200 in the new South Hills Village parking garage.

How many gallons of fuel does the Port Authority fleet consume in a year?

10 million gallons.

How many people ride Port Authority trolleys, buses, and inclines each year?

In 2004, Port Authority carried 67.8 million passengers. About 58.4 million of the total rode the buses.

How many passengers does Port Authority carry on a typical day?

240,000.

How many different transit routes does Port Authority operate?

206.

You can ride a bus over how many miles of Port Authority busways?

18.4.

How long is the Port Authority's Martin Luther King Jr. East Busway Extension?

2.3 miles. It runs from Wilkinsburg to the Swissvale-Rankin boundary and took 15 years to build at a cost of $68.8 million. It opened in June 2003.

Which of Port Authority's busways is the longest?

It's the East Busway, which runs 9.1 miles. The West Busway is 5.0 miles, and the South Busway is 4.3 miles.

How many transit stops does Port Authority have?

15,742.

When Port Authority started operating in 1964, how many different bus and trolley companies did it consolidate?

33. The largest was the Pittsburgh Railways Company.

How many people land and take off from the Pittsburgh International Airport?

In 2005, 10.4+ million passengers landed and took off from Pittsburgh International Airport; 59% were USAirways passengers and 6% were Southwest. In 2004, 13.3 million passengers either got on or got off airplanes at the airport. USAirways accounted for 76 percent of the passengers. In 1999, 19.6 million passengers got on or off airplanes, and US Airways had 87% of the business.

How fast do the moving sidewalks at the Pittsburgh International Airport move?

They move 125 feet per minute. Of the 20 moving sidewalks at the airport, the longest is 365 feet.

How many flights go in and out of Pittsburgh International Airport each day?

In June, 2006, the daily average was 268 flights; an average of 334 went out throughout 2004. In 1999, the figure was 1,119.

How long is the longest runway at the Pittsburgh International Airport?

11,500 feet.

What percentage of all flights arrive and depart the Pittsburgh International Airport on time?

In February 2005, 75.66 percent arrived on time and 84.55 percent departed on time. The airport ranked 16th nationally for arrivals and 6th in departures.

What is the Federal Aviation Administration's three-character airport code for the Pittsburgh International Airport? For the Allegheny County Airport in West Mifflin?

PIT and AGC. The code for the Arnold Palmer Regional Airport in Latrobe is LBE.

On July 19, 1914, at the corner of Smithfield Street and Sixth Avenue in downtown Pittsburgh, the first of its kind in the state, maybe in the country, was installed. What was it?

An automatic streetlight.

How safe from vehicular traffic are pedestrians on Pittsburgh-area streets?

Very. A Washington, DC study group (Environmental Working Group) rates Pittsburgh second safest behind Boston, MA. The group studied 47 metropolitan areas with a population of a million or more. The study covers 2002 to 2003.

What are the Pittsburgh area's busiest intersections?

Routes 22 and 48 in Monroeville with 70,000 vehicles a day and the Liberty Tunnels at Route 51 with 60,000 a day.

What streets rank as the steepest in Pittsburgh?

Street, neighborhood (degree of incline): E. Woodford, Carrick (27.6 degrees); Cutler, North Side/Perrysville (26 degrees); SoHo, Uptown (24.7 degrees); Rialto, North Side/E. Ohio (24 degrees); Hampshire Avenue, Beechview (22.7 degrees); Estella, Mount Washington (20 degrees).

Phoenix, Arizona leads the nation in deaths caused by drivers running red lights. What is Pittsburgh's standing?

In American cities with a population of 200,000 or more, Pittsburgh was second-safest behind Columbus, Ohio. The study was done between 1992 and 1998. The Institute of Highway Safety says only two deaths were reported in Pittsburgh. Phoenix had 122. Pittsburgh had 0.6 deaths per 100,000 people. Phoenix had 10.8 deaths per 100,000 people. Those killed were either pedestrians or occupants of other vehicles.

How many road service calls does the West Penn AAA get a year?

A little over one million. The West Penn AAA, founded in 1903, handles Western Pennsylvania, and parts of Ohio, West Virginia and western New York.

Where are the biggest parking lot and garage in the city of Pittsburgh?

The biggest lot is on Reedsdale Street near the new stadia. It holds 1,100 vehicles. The biggest garage is Allegheny Center, also on the North Side. It holds about 2,700 vehicles.

Once the trails are completed (hopefully in the next decade), you will be able to walk or bike from Pittsburgh 334.5 miles to what city south of Pittsburgh?

Washington, DC. The trail will have two parts: The Great Allegheny Passage (Pittsburgh to Cumberland, MD) and the C&O Canal Tow Path (Cumberland, MD to its end in the Georgetown neighborhood of Washington).

How many local drivers by county are vain enough to get vanity license plates?

Allegheny, 22,322 (Allegheny County leads the state with the most vanity plates); Beaver, 3,622; Butler, 3,969; Fayette, 2,760; Washington, 4,429; Westmoreland, 7,992.

How much money did the city of Pittsburgh plan to spend on salt on roads in the winter of 2005-2006?

About $1,070,000. That's just for salt. Labor is extra. It costs the city $60,000, in salt and labor, to handle one inch of snow.

In the city of Pittsburgh in 2004, how many traffic tickets were issued?

Parking tickets: 293,379 (meter enforcement officers issued 252,883 tickets; police officers, 40,496). Moving violations: 24,450.

How many licensed motorcycles are in the six-county Pittsburgh area?

53,954.

If you are looking for a parking space in the city of Pittsburgh, how many spaces in lots and garages do you have to choose from?

There are about 79,200 parking spaces in Pittsburgh lots and garages.

How many passenger vehicles are registered in the six-county Pittsburgh area?

As of the end of 2004: 1,396,215. By county: Allegheny, 714,810; Beaver, 107,137; Butler, 132,523; Fayette, 87,357; Washington, 127,928; Westmoreland, 226,460.

How many licensed drivers are there in the Pittsburgh area?

As of 2004, 1,959,915. By county, that's Allegheny, 923,165; Beaver, 158,847; Butler, 205,733; Fayette, 110,613; Washington, 152,504; Westmoreland, 270,830.

How many taxicabs are licensed by the state to operate in Allegheny County?

310. Cabs licensed in other counties: Beaver, 9; Butler, 3; Fayette, 8; Washington, 19; Westmoreland, 34.

How many "incidents" (flat tires, breakdowns, accidents, running out of gas), on average, occur in the Fort Pitt Tunnels in a given week?

28.

There are five beltways circling Allegheny County. It may be the only highway system in the U.S. that is color-coded instead of having names or numbers. What are the colors and why were they chosen?

The county developed the system in the 1940s prior to the interstate system, choosing colors in the rainbow. A color's location in the rainbow is an indication of how far a driver is from the center of the county. The beltways' colors are: blue, green, yellow, orange, and red. Blue is the innermost beltway.

How much did it cost to hop on a Port Authority bus or trolley in early 1980? How much more to hop on by 2002?

In 1980 the basic fare was 60 cents. The fare went to $1.75 by 2002, and that's still the fare.

How is it possible to go between Beaver County and Lawrence County without crossing over a county line?

By going through a railroad tunnel that connects Franklin Township (Beaver) with Ellwood City (Lawrence).

Where was the first drive-in gasoline station in the United States?
Gulf Oil opened the first station on December 1, 1913 at the intersection of Baum Boulevard and Saint Clair Street in the East Liberty section of Pittsburgh. Gas was 27 cents a gallon and the free Gulf road maps were also first distributed there.

In 2004, Port Authority of Allegheny County re-opened the Wabash Tunnel connecting Route 51 in the South Hills to West Carson Street. How long is the tunnel, when was it built and when was it closed?

3,450 feet long, 1903, 1946.

The Road Information Program (TRIP) in Washington, DC is a non-profit organization that researches and evaluates highway transportation issues. In 2005 the group came out with a report that rates "the roughest rides on roads." How did Pittsburgh do in the report?

TRIP says that 22% of Pittsburgh's roads are poor, 39% are mediocre, 23% are fair, and 15% are good. The report is based on the level of smoothness of pavement surfaces and ride quality. The survey includes interstates and heavily traveled commuter roads. TRIP says the condition of Pittsburgh's roads adds $370 annually to the cost of operating a car here. The roads in San Jose, California had the highest poor rating: 67%. Eighty-three percent of Orlando's (Florida) roads were good—the best rating of any city.

Food (and Drink) for Thought

Don't hold the fries! Courtesy of Primanti Brothers Restaurant.

Where was the first Eat 'n Park located?

On Route 51 South, not too far from the Liberty Tunnels. The spot is now the location of another restaurant. The 13-seat store opened in 1949 with ten carhops. The second store opened in Avalon.

Where did McDonald's sell its first Big Mac?

The first worldwide sale of a Big Mac took place at McDonald's Uniontown store on Morgantown Street in 1968. It sold for 49 cents. Jim Delligatti, a Pittsburgh McDonald's franchisee, invented the Big Mac.

The first Wendy's opened in Pittsburgh in 1976. Where?

At the intersection of Routes 30 and 48 in North Versailles. It's still there.

When were Klondikes invented and who invented them?

In 1929, by Sam Isaly. For the unaware, Klondikes are squares of ice cream dipped in chocolate and wrapped in a silver wrapper. They are still sold today, although the company was sold several years ago.

To a romanticist, Isaly's was more than a place to buy ice cream. What did the letters in Isaly's stand for?

Isaly's also stood for "I shall always love you."

How many inches high was an Isaly's Skyscraper ice cream cone?

The cone was five inches high. The ice cream was about six inches high for a total of 11 inches.

What brewery made the Prince of Pilsners and Silver Top beer?

Duquesne Brewery on Pittsburgh's South Side. The company was also famous for the massive "Have a Duke" clock on the side of its plant.

Where is the farthest away from Pittsburgh that you can buy a bottle of Rolling Rock beer?

Currently, Hawaii or Alaska (Rolling Rock is sold in all 50 states). In the past, the little green bottles have gone as far as Japan. Unfortunately, as of July 2006, brewing has moved to New Jersey.

Mario's South Side Saloon in Pittsburgh sells beer by the yard. That is, you can buy 42 ounces of beer served in a yard-high glass. If you can drink 100 yards of beer, you score a touchdown. Since Mario's opened in November 1982, how many touchdowns has the leading beer drinker scored?

Ten plus, or 1,014 yards of beer over a 14-year period.

When was the first time beer was sold at a Pittsburgh sporting event?

July 16, 1970 at the opening of Three Rivers Stadium. Iron City sold for 50 cents. The other brands were 10 cents more.

In 1984, a popular Pittsburgh restaurant burned. This restaurant was a boat docked on the Monongahela River adjacent to the Mon Wharf, directly across from Station Square. What was the restaurant's name?

The Pilot House. The restaurant was built on two barges in 1965.

How many sandwiches does Primanti Brothers in the Strip District sell each week?

Approximately 8,000 in a good week.

What goes into the making of a Primanti Brothers sandwich?

Your choice of meat, coleslaw, tomatoes, french fries and provolone cheese.

How many pounds of french fries are sold at Oakland's Original Hot Dog Shop each week?

43,000 pounds. Hot dogs? 2,000-3,000 a day!

Who designed the Devonshire sandwich and the pecan ball?

The credit goes to Frank Blandi, who operated the LeMont Restaurant on top of Pittsburgh's Mount Washington overlooking the Golden Triangle. The name "Devonshire" was chosen because that was the name of a street near a restaurant owned by Blandi.

Which local brewer was crowned the maker of the best dark beer in the world in 2000?

Penn Brewery on Pittsburgh's North Side. Every other year there is an international, Olympic-style beer competition. Penn Brewery's "Penn Dark" won the gold medal for best dark beer at the World Beer International Competition. It is the roasting of the malt that makes the beer dark.

How many establishments (both for profit and nonprofit) are licensed by the state to sell beer and liquor in the City of Pittsburgh? In Allegheny County?

City, 698 (16 can sell beer only); county, 2,051(27 can sell beer only). The county figures include the city.

Where in the world is the world's largest mushroom farm?

It is Moonlight Mushrooms, Inc., which is in Worthington, PA, about 35 miles northeast of Pittsburgh in Armstrong County. The farm has 156 miles of underground galleries and produces over 50 million pounds of mushrooms a year. The site is an old limestone mine.

Sunday brunch at the Grand Concourse attracts an average of how many people each week?

800.

PL&E Railroad waiting room at Station Square, now the Grand Concourse restaurant. Library of Congress, Historic American Buildings Survey. HABS PA, 2-PITBU, 55-1. Photographer and date unknown.

The Gandy Dancer is a restaurant located in the old Pittsburgh and Lake Erie passenger station, which is now part of Station Square. What is a Gandy Dancer?

Two explanations. One is that an Irishman by the name of Gandy was the boss of the immigrants who built the railroad to California. The other is that railroad workers used tools made by Gandy Manufacturing of Chicago.

North Side druggist E. J. W. Keagy never was a household name, but his creation showed up in thousands of households. What did Keagy create?

In 1914, he came up with a lemon-flavored ice slush beverage and called it Lem-N-Blennd. A candy company, Reymer's and Bros. Inc., bought the right to Lem-N-Blennd in 1932 and the product became Reymer's Lem-N-Blennd.

What is the best-selling cheesecake at the South Side Works' Cheesecake Factory?

The white chocolate raspberry truffle. There are over 35 different cheesecakes sold there. Nationally, fresh strawberry cheesecake is the Cheesecake Factory's number one seller.

PUCKS, BALLS, BATS, JOCKS, PONIES
AND ALL THAT OTHER STUFF

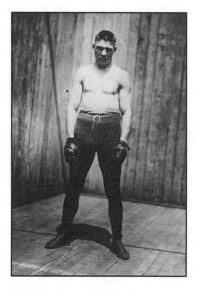

The Pittsburgh Windmill. Courtesy of the Carnegie Library of Pittsburgh.

The University of Pittsburgh chose the panther as its mascot in 1909. What specific species of panther was chosen as the mascot?

Felis Concolor. *The school could have just as easily chosen* Panthera Pardus *or* Panthera Pardalis.

Which area athlete has appeared on the cover of *Sports Illustrated* the most times?

Arnold Palmer has been on the SI's cover 13 times, more than any other golfer. Evidently, Palmer is not a victim of the Sports Illustrated *cover jinx or the number 13.*

Who were the only Pittsburgh-born athletes to win medals at the Olympics?

There have been only two. Pitt track star Herb Douglas won the bronze in the long jump in 1948. He jumped 24 feet, 8 3/9 inches. Suzie McConnell Serio won two medals in basketball in 1988 and 1992.

Who is the only athlete to have played with the Steelers and the Pirates?

Rex Johnston. He was a running back with the Steelers in 1960 and a Pirates' outfielder in 1964.

The Stadiums (or stadia for you purists)

What teams played in the first college football game at Three Rivers Stadium?

On September 12, 1970, Grambling College of Louisiana, played Morgan State of Baltimore. Grambling 38, Morgan State 12.

How much does the Sony Jumbotron scoreboard and video display at the Mellon Arena weigh? How big is it and how much did it cost?

About 36,000 pounds. It cost $34 million and has four, eight-foot by 10-foot screens. Each of the big screens is made up of 120 mini-screens. It was installed in 1995.

Which stadium cost more to build: PNC Park or Heinz Field?

PNC Park cost $270,776,326 followed by Heinz Field at $261,089,461. Ketchup flows slower than cash.

Why is the chance of a frozen turf at Heinz Field a very low probability?

The field has an underground heating system. When the area below the sod dips below 60 degrees, the heating system is activated. The system has 35 miles of tubing.

What team won the first football game played at Heinz Field?

Pitt beat East Tennessee State 31-0, on September 1, 2001. David Priestly scored the first touchdown on an 85-yard run at 8:30 of the first quarter.

At Heinz Field, how far are the sidelines from the front row seats? How far from the end zones are the front row seats?

The sidelines are 60 feet from the seats and the end zones are 25 feet away.

PNC Park. Courtesy of the Pittsburgh Pirates.

In its 100+ year history, how many major owners have the Pirates had?

Barney Dreyfuss (1900-1932), Bill Benswager (1932-August 8, 1946), John Galbreath (August 8, 1946—October 2, 1985), Pittsburgh Associates (October 2, 1985—February 14, 1996), Kevin McClatchy (February 14, 1996—present), and G. Ogden Nutting and Bob Nutting (1996—present). There are also over twenty limited partners.

Did the Pirates win or lose the first game played at PNC Park?

They lost to the Reds, 8-2, on April 9, 2001.

Since the Pirates threw out the first pitch in 1887, how many home parks have they had and what were their names?

Five: Recreation Park, Exposition Park, Forbes Field (Oakland), Three Rivers Stadium (North Shore), and PNC Park (North Shore). Recreation Park and Exposition Park were located near Three Rivers and PNC Park.

Fill in the distances from home plate at PNC Park to the following locations: (a) Right field foul line, (b) right field power alley, (c) center field, (d) outfield deepest point, (e) left field power alley, (f) left field foul line.

(a) 320 feet, (b) 375 feet, (c) 399 feet, (d) 410 feet, (e) 389 feet, (f) 325 feet.

A baseball fan sitting in the last row behind home plate at PNC Park is how far from home plate?

88 feet. At Three Rivers Stadium, the comparable distance was 132 feet.

The right field wall at PNC Park has a symbolic height. What is that height and why was it planned that way?

It is 21 feet high in honor of Roberto Clemente, who wore 21 on his uniform.

How far is it from the PNC Park home plate to Allegheny River?

443 feet, four inches.

What variety of grass covers the playing field at PNC Park?

Kentucky bluegrass.

How many "potties" are available at PNC Park?

265 for women; 230 toilets or urinals for men.

BASEBALL

Who was the only sitting U.S. president to watch a major league baseball game in Pittsburgh?

President William Howard Taft, who served in the early 1900s. He saw two games: one at Exposition Field on Pittsburgh's North Side and one at Forbes Field.

How did the Pittsburgh Pirates get their name?

By being pirates, of course. The team signed a second baseman, Louis Bierbauer, from another team for play in the 1891 season. Other teams in baseball started calling the Pittsburgh team "Pirates" for their shenanigans. Previously, the Pirates were the Pittsburgh Alleghenies.

Only three Pirates have hit 30 or more home runs in three consecutive seasons. Name them.

Ralph Kiner, Willie Stargell, Brian Giles.

How many no-hitters were thrown at the old Forbes Field?

None. The park's configuration didn't treat pitchers kindly.

Where and when was the first World Series night game played?

At Three Rivers Stadium on October 3, 1971, when the Bucs took on the Baltimore Orioles. The Bucs won 4-3.

Baseball Hall of Fame member, Stan Musial, and Cincinnati Reds Golden Glover, Ken Griffey, Jr., each bat left-handed. What else do they have in common?

Each was born in Donora, Pennsylvania.

When and how did "The Great One," Pirates' right fielder Roberto Clemente, die?

He died in a plane crash on New Year's Eve in 1972. Clemente was on his way to help earthquake victims in Nicaragua.

Roberto Clemente ended his Pirates' career wearing number 21. What was his original number?

13.

Which Pirates' pitcher is the team career leader in innings pitched (3,481), losses (218), strikeouts (1,682) and walks (869)?

Bob Friend.

How many Pittsburgh Pirates are in the Baseball Hall of Fame?

Twelve players.

Which Pirates' alumnus was among the first five players elected to the Baseball Hall of Fame in 1936?

Shortstop Honus Wagner.

Batting helmets are now commonplace in baseball. In the 1950s they were less common than a no-hitter. What Pittsburgher helped to create the helmets?

It was Charlie Muse, a Pittsburgh Pirates executive for 52 years, serving as the team's traveling secretary for many of those years. Muse, along with two other men, designed a helmet for Branch Rickey, the Bucs' general manager. The Pirates were the first team to wear the helmets in 1952. Prior to plastic helmets a player's only protection was the cloth cap. Muse died in 2005.

Which Pittsburgh Pirate pitched a no-hitter while on LSD?

Dock Ellis. He beat San Diego in 1970. The Pirates won 2-0, but Dock walked 8 batters. He recounted his trip in a 1993 interview in San Francisco.

Where and when did Babe Ruth hit his last home run?

Forbes Field on May 25, 1935. In fact, Babe hit three home runs that day. The last one, his career 714th, went over the right field roof. No one ever did that before at Forbes Field.

What were the names of the two Pittsburgh area black professional baseball teams?

The Homestead Grays and the Pittsburgh Crawfords.

Who was the first player to hit a home run at Three Rivers Stadium?

Tony Perez from the Cincinnati Reds with one on base in the fifth inning on July 16, 1970.

Which Pittsburgh outfielder led or shared in leading the National League in home runs each of the seven years he played for the Bucs?

Ralph Kiner, who played between 1946 and 1952.

How many innings was the longest baseball game ever played at Three Rivers Stadium?

Twenty innings on July 6, 1980 against the Chicago Cubs. The Bucs won 5-4. There was a 21 inning game at Forbes Field against the New York Giants in 1914. Bucs lost 3-1.

Who was the winning pitcher in the seventh game when the Pirates won the 1960 World Series? Who was the starting pitcher?

Harvey Haddix won. Vernon Law was the starting pitcher.

Who were the seventh-game winning pitchers when the Pirates won the 1971 and 1979 World Series?

1971—Steve Blass; 1979—Grant Jackson.

On what date was the last game played at Forbes Field?

June 28, 1970.

At Forbes Field, how far was it down the left field and right field foul lines? What was the distance to the center field wall?

It was 300 feet to the right, 365 to the left. The deepest part of the center field was 462 feet.

Where were the "Greenberg Gardens?"

At Forbes Field. The Pirates' owners built a fence on the playing field, extending from left field towards center so that sluggers Hank Greenberg and Ralph Kiner would have an easier time hitting home runs over a shorter distance.

When was the first Pirates' baseball game broadcast on radio?

August 6, 1921 on KDKA Radio. The Bucs beat Philadelphia 8-5 at Forbes Field.

What were the names of the two watch companies that advertised on the Forbes Field scoreboard?

Gruen and Longines Wittnauer.

What is the record for Pirates' season attendance?

2,436,139 in 2001 at PNC Park. The highest Pirates' attendance at Forbes Field was 1,705,828 in 1960. For Three Rivers, the highest season attendance was 2,065,302 (1991).

Against which pitcher did Pirates' slugger Roberto Clemente get his first hit and against which pitcher did he get his 3,000th hit, which was his last?

First hit against John Padres of the Brooklyn Dodgers. The 3,000th and last hit was against John Matlack of the New York Mets.

Who is the only major league baseball player to hit home runs in three consecutive All-Star games?

Ralph Kiner in 1949-50-51.

Who was the last Pirates' pitcher to start an All-Star game for the National League?

Dock Ellis in 1971.

Who was the first African American to play for the Pittsburgh Pirates?

Curt Roberts. He started at second base on opening day, April 13, 1954.

How many Pirates have been named Rookie of the Year since the award was started in 1947 by the Baseball Writers of America?

Only one, Jason Bay in 2004. Bay is also the only native Canadian to win the award.

Which Pittsburgh Pirates' player invented the "eephus" pitch?

Pitcher Rip Sewell who played for the Pirates in the 1940s. The pitch has an arc of about 25 feet between the mound and the home plate and it is thrown overhand. It is also called a lob. Sewell first threw the pitch in 1942.

Which Pirates' player shares the major league record for hitting at least one home run in the most consecutive games?

Dale Long hit a home run in eight consecutive games in 1956. Long shares the record with the Yankees' Don Mattingly (1987), and Seattle's Ken Griffey Jr. (1993).

Which Pirates' player has the record for the most consecutive games with at least one RBI?

In 1927, Paul Waner had 12 consecutive games with at least one RBI.

Which Pirates' player set the major league record for consecutive times at bat (918) without hitting into a double play?

Tony Womack set the record in 1997-98 over a period of 220 games.

Which Pirates' player has the team record for consecutive steals without getting caught?

Tony Womack. He stole 32 straight bases in 1997.

Since 1900, only three shortstops have won National League batting championships and all are Pirates. Who are they?

Dick Groat (1960), Arky Vaughn (1935), and Honus Wagner (8 times: 1900, 1903, 1904, 1906, 1907, 1908, 1909, 1911).

What are the most games the Pirates have won in a single season?

110 in 1909. They went 110-42 for a .724 percentage. They went 95-58 in 1925. In modern times, they won 95 games in 1960.

What are the most games the Pirates have lost in a single season?

103 in 1890 and 112 in 1952.

In more than 17,000 games, how many times have the Pirates led off a game with back-to-back home runs?

Twice. Once in 1945, the other time in 1982.

How many Pirates have hit home runs their first time at bat in the major leagues?

Two. Walter Mueller in 1922, and Don Leppert in 1961.

How many different Pirates have led the National League in home runs?

Only three. Willie Stargell led the league twice, Ralph Kiner seven times, and Tommy Leach once.

Since the turn of the 20th century, what team has had more batting champions than any other major league franchise?

The Pirates with 24.

Which Pirates' player has the most pinch hits?

Willie Stargell with 55.

Who is the only Pirates' manager to be named major league manager of the year by the *Sporting News*?

Danny Murtaugh in 1960.

How many Pittsburgh Pirates have won Gold Glove Awards?

14.

Who are the only Pirates to hit left-handed and right-handed home runs in the same game?

Bobby Bonilla (1987 and 1988) and Dale Sveum (1999).

The main entrance to Forbes Field was at the intersection of what two streets?

Bouquet and Sennott.

The same pitcher has the most wins and the most losses at Three Rivers Stadium. Who is he?

John Candelaria, who has won 60 games and lost 47.

Which Pirates' player hit the most home runs at Three Rivers Stadium?

Willie Stargell with 147.

Which opposing player hit the most home runs at Three Rivers Stadium?

Mike Schmidt with 25 home runs.

Which Pirates' player has the National League record for season steals by a catcher?

Jason Kendall, who stole 26 bases in 1998. Kendall is only one of four catchers to steal at least 20 bases twice in a career.

How many times have the Pirates hit three consecutive home runs in one inning?

Only seven times. The last time was in 1995.

Who was the last major league pitcher to pitch 18 innings in *one* game?

Pirates' player Vernon Law on July 19, 1955 against the Milwaukee Braves. The Pirates won 4-3 in 19 innings. Law got a no-decision.

How many players have hit for the cycle at Three Rivers Stadium?

Only three: Joe Torre in 1973, Jeff Kent in 1999, and Jason Kendall in 2000. To "hit for the cycle" is to hit a single, double, triple and home run in the same game. To do so in order is termed a "natural cycle." In the history of the Pirates going back to 1887, only 20 different players have hit for the cycle, doing it 23 times.

What is the only team to win a World Series without a pitcher who won at least 15 games and a hitter who drove in at least 100 RBI?

1979 Pirates.

How many times has a Pirates' pitcher struck out the side on nine pitches?

Once. Jeff Robinson did it in 1987, tying a major league record.

Who are the all-time Pittsburgh Pirates' leaders in the following categories: doubles, triples, home runs, hits, games, at bats, extra base hits, runs, runs batted in?

Doubles (556), triples (231), home runs (975), hits (3,000), games (2,433), at bats (9,459), extra base hits (953), runs (1,520), runs batted in (1,540). Roberto Clemente leads in at bats, hits and games. Honus Wagner leads in doubles, triples and runs. Willie Stargell leads in home runs, extra base hits and runs batted in.

*The greatest walk-off home run ever. Courtesy
of the Carnegie Library of Pittsburgh.*

Here is a grand slam question: What time was showing on the score-board clock at Forbes Field when Bill Mazeroski hit his 1960 World Series home run? What company's name is advertised on the clock? What was the count on Mazeroski and who was on deck?

3:36; Longines Wittnauer; 1-0; Dick Stuart.

Willie Stargell hit how many home runs over the right-field roof at Forbes Field?

Seven. In 45 years only 18 homers went over the roof.

How many Pirates' pitchers have won the Cy Young award, representing the best national league pitcher in a given season?

Two. Vernon Law in 1960 and Doug Drabek in 1990.

Only two baseball players not only won the batting championships, but also struck out more than 100 times. They both played for the Pirates. Who were they?

Roberto Clemente in 1967 and Dave Parker in 1977.

How many no-hitters were pitched at Three Rivers Stadium?

Three. Saint Louis Cardinal Bob Gibson, won 11-0 in 1971 and Pirate John Candelaria beat the Dodgers 2-0 in 1976. Francisco Cordova and Ricardo Rincon combined for a 10-inning no-hitter in 1997. Bucs won 3-0.

What baseball game attracted the largest crowd to ever see a game at Three Rivers Stadium?

The July 12, 1994 All-Star game had 59,568 fans in the stands. The largest crowd to see a game at Forbes Field was 44,932, for the Bucs vs. Brooklyn on September 23, 1956.

Which team drew the largest regular season crowd for a baseball game at Three Rivers Stadium?

The Montreal Expos played the Pirates before 54,274 fans on April 8, 1991.

Today, where can you find Forbes Field's home plate located in its original location?

On the first floor of the University of Pittsburgh's Wesley W. Posvar Hall.

Pittsburgh numbers racketeer, William Greenlee, owned what baseball team in the 1930s?

The Pittsburgh Crawfords of the Negro National League.

In 2002, who was the first player to hit a home run out of PNC Park into the Allegheny River on the fly?

The Houston Astros' Daryle Ward. The ball traveled about 479 feet.

In the spring of 1985, numerous major league baseball players stepped off the field to play a little defense in a Pittsburgh courtroom. Those testifying at a well-publicized federal trial were: Dave Parker, Rod Scurry, Dale Berry, Keith Hernandez, Lonnie Smith and Enos Cabell. Even the Pirate Parrot took the stand (presumably in civilian clothes). Why such an impressive witness lineup?

They were called to testify at the "Pittsburgh drug trials." Seven individuals were convicted on various charges – none of them ball players, but the trials brought out evidence of the extent of cocaine abuse among major league players.

How many Pirates' pitchers have thrown no-hitters?

Nick Maddox in 1907, Cliff Chambers in 1951, Harvey Haddix in 1953, Bob Moose in 1969, Dock Ellis in 1970, John Candelaria in 1976, and Francisco Cordova and Ricardo Rincon in 1997 (a combined effort).

Where is the Pony League (ages 13-14) World Series held each year?

In Washington, PA. The first Pony League World Series was in 1952; a team from San Antonio, Texas won. In 1959, the first team from outside the U.S. participated in the series. They came from Monterrey, Mexico.

Who was the only player to hit a home run over the 457-foot mark at Forbes Field?

Dick Stuart on June 5, 1959.

When is the last time a Pirates' player went seven for seven in a game?

Rennie Stennett did it on August 16, 1975 against the Chicago Cubs. He hit two doubles, one triple and four singles.

Who are the youngest and oldest Pirates to hit home runs?

Bobby Del Greco (19) and Honus Wagner (42).

Which Pittsburgh pitcher holds the record for most losses in a single season?

Murray Dickson, who lost 21 games in 1952.

During the 1995 season, the Pirates had two sets of brothers on the roster, including identical twins. Who were they?

Gene and George Freese, and twins Johnny and Eddie O'Brien.

In a September 1, 1971 game against the Philadelphia Phillies, here was the Pirates' starting lineup: 2B, Rennie Stennett; CF, Gene Clines; RF, Roberto Clemente; LF, Willie Stargell; C, Manny Sanguillen; 3B, Dave Cash; 1B, Al Oliver; SS, Jackie Hernandez; P, Dock Ellis. Why did this lineup make Major League Baseball history?

It was the first all-black and Latino lineup in an MLB game. Regular third baseman Richie Hebner was out with an injury; regular first baseman Bob Robertson had a rest day. The lineup lasted only one inning because Ellis was taken out in the second.

BASKETBALL

Match these NBA players with the Western Pennsylvania high schools they attended: (1) Armon Gillam, (2) Billy Knight, (3) Norm Van Lear, (4) Brad Davis, (5) Mickey Davis, (6) Dennis Wuycik and (A) Monaca, (B) Ambridge, (C) Midland, (D) General Braddock, (E) Bethel Park.

1=E, 2=D, 3=C, 4 and 5 =A, 6 = B

W hat's the largest crowd to ever watch a basketball game in the city of Pittsburgh?

17,716 fans saw Pitt play North Carolina on December 20, 1993 at the Civic/Mellon Arena. On March 16, 1989 there were 37,242 fans in the stands for a match between Pitt and Ball State in Indianapolis. That game set Pitt's single-game attendance record.

P itt basketball great Don Hennon played in 76 games between 1956 and 1959. In how many of those 76 games did he score in double figures?

78. He also scored 20-plus points in 52 games.

I n 1988, two Pitt basketball players were chosen in the first round of the NBA draft for the only time in Pitt's history. Who were they?

Charles Smith and Jerome Lane. Smith is also Pitt's highest NBA draft pick—third overall.

H ow many father and son combinations have ever played basketball at the University of Pittsburgh?

Only two. Samuel David (1945-49) and Joey David (1983-86); and Brian Generalovich (1961-64) and Brock Generalovich (1989-93). There have been eight different brother combinations in Pitt's basketball history.

H ow many All-American basketball players have played for Duquesne University?

Seven: Paul Birch, 1935; Chuck Cooper, 1950; Herb Bonn, 1936; Dick Ricketts, 1955; Moe Becker, 1941; Sihugo Green, 1955-56; Willie Somerset, 1965.

Who were the "Iron Dukes?"

The 1939-40 Duquesne University basketball team, which depended on its five resilient starters to win games. In the 1939-40 season, the "Iron Dukes" went 20 to 3 and even made it to the finals of the National Invitational Tournament in Madison Square Garden in New York City.

For what Pittsburgh professional basketball team did Connie Hawkins play?

The six-foot, eight-inch Hawkins played for the Pittsburgh Pipers in the American Basketball Association. He never played college ball because he was rumored to have ties to gamblers. He did get into the NBA, however, with the Phoenix Suns.

What is the only Pittsburgh team to ever win a pro-basketball title?

The Pittsburgh Pipers won the American Basketball Association title during the 1967-68 season. Believe it or not, the seventh and final game of the championship drew over 11,000 fans at the Civic Arena.

Who was the first black basketball player to be drafted into the National Basketball Association?

Chuck Cooper, a 1950 Duquesne University All-American, played for the Boston Celtics.

What was the last year Pitt had a perfect season in men's basketball, going 21 and 0?

In 1928. Pitt's team was the first major college team to have a perfect record.

Which Pitt Panther basketball players have: The best career field goal percentage; the best career free throw percentage; the most career rebounds?

Best field goal percentage career: Brian Shorter (1988-91)—.538 percent. Best free throw percentage career: Sean Miller (1987-92)—.885 percent. Most career rebounds: Sam Clancy (1977-81)—1,342.

Which man started his coaching career at Punxsutawney High School and eventually led the Detroit Pistons to an NBA championship?

Chuck Daly. The Pistons won in 1990.

Which University of Pittsburgh assistant basketball coach devised the "amoeba defense?" (The amoeba is a switching defense that mixes zone and man-to-man coverage. It's called amoeba because it changes its shape.)

Fran Webster (1969-1975).

In the first men's basketball game at the Petersen Events Center in November 2002, which Pitt player: (a) made the first field goal? (b) had the first field goal attempt? (c) made the first free throw? (d) blocked the first shot?

Ontario Lett (a,b,d). Julius Page (c). Lett also snagged the first rebound.

Which two teams played in the first basketball game at the University of Pittsburgh's Petersen Events Center?

Pitt's Lady Panthers beat Robert Morris 90-51 on November 22, 2002.

Who was the first African American to play basketball for the University of Pittsburgh?

Julius Pegues who played between 1954-58.

Football: High School

What high school did future NFL (San Francisco 49ers and Kansas City Chiefs) Hall of Famer Joe Montana attend?

Ringgold High School in Washington County. In his earlier years, Montana tossed a football at the Park Avenue playground in Monongahela.

New Kensington's Willie Thrower is famous for doing what?

On October 18, 1953 he became the first African American to play quarterback in the NFL. Thrower attended Michigan State and was the first African American to play quarterback at a Big Ten school.

What does "WPIAL" stand for and when was it formed?

The Western Pennsylvania Interscholastic Athletic League was formed in 1906. The league organizes and develops athletics for junior and senior high schools in Western Pennsylvania.

What school won the first WPIAL football championship?

Wilkinsburg, in 1914. The school was the champ in 1915 and 1916, too.

What school has won the most WPIAL football championships?

Aliquippa with 12. New Castle is next with 10.

Which WPIAL football player has gained the most rushing yards?

Mike Vernillo, who graduated from Fort Cherry in 1999, gained 6,625 yards in 825 attempts throughout his high school career.

What WPIAL school has the longest unbeaten streak in football?

Braddock. Between 1953 and 1960 the school was 55-0-1.

Who is the first WPIAL football coach to win in 300 games?

Jim Render, the football coach at Upper Saint Clair, won his 300th game in 2005. It took him 37 years of coaching to reach that milestone. Eight other active WPIAL coaches have won more than 200 games.

Which three Heisman Trophy winners played their high school football in Western Pennsylvania?

Tony Dorsett, Leon Hart and John Lujack.

What Pittsburgh city school has won the most football champion-ships?

Starting in 1919, Westinghouse has won 35 championships, including eight in a row (1954-61).

Which Western Pennsylvania star athlete said, "I can't wait until tomorrow . . . 'cause I get better looking everyday?"

That modest statement comes from Beaver Falls' Joe Namath. Joe left Beaver Falls to star at the University of Alabama and for the New York Jets as a quarterback. The quote comes from the title of his autobiography, published in 1969.

FOOTBALL: COLLEGE

This area college now competes in NCAA Division III football. In 1922, the school was in the Rose Bowl, the smallest school ever to be invited. What's the college's name?

Washington & Jefferson College. It played the University of California to a scoreless tie, the only scoreless tie in Rose Bowl history. Washington & Jefferson played with only 11 men and no substitutes.

Which 1947 Notre Dame Heisman Trophy winner was born in Connellsville?

Jonny Lujack graduated from Connellsville High School in 1941. He led Notre Dame to a 9 and 0 season in 1947. After college, he played with the Chicago Bears for four years. With the Bears, he made as much as $20,000 a year.

Which ex-University of Pittsburgh football coach had three of his players serve simultaneously as head coaches in the National Football League?

John Michelosen, who coached from 1955 to 1966. Michelosen's players-turned-coaches included: Mike Ditka (Chicago Bears); Joe Walton (New York Jets); and Marty Schottenheimer (Kansas City Chiefs).

In how many years were there three Pitt Panther football players drafted in the first round in the NFL draft?

Two. 1981 and 1983.

How many times has the Pitt football team been declared national champions?

9 times: 1915-16, 1918, 1929, 1931, 1934, 1936-37 and 1976.

W ho is the only player in the history of football to win the Heisman Trophy, a collegiate National Championship, a Super Bowl Championship, and be inducted into the College and Pro Football Halls of Fame?

Tony Dorsett. The Pitt All-American played for the Dallas Cowboys from 1977 to 1987 and finished his pro career with the Denver Broncos, 1988-89.

W hat was the largest crowd ever to watch a Pitt football game at Pitt Stadium?

In 1938, 68,918 people saw Pitt play Fordham. Pitt beat Fordham 24-13.

P ittsburgh pro quarterbacks Dan Marino and John Unitas both lost Super Bowls for the same coach and they also have the same middle name. Who is the coach and what is Marino's and Unitas' middle name?

Don Shula and Constantine.

W hich of these football players was not a member of the 1938 University of Pittsburgh "Dream Backfield:" Marshall Goldberg, Dick Cassiano, Len Casanova, Harold Stebbins, John Chicherneo?

Casanova coached for a very short time at Pitt, but he never spent time in the backfield.

T he day was January 1, 1937. The place was Pasadena, California. The score of the football game was University of Pittsburgh 21, Washington 0. What was significant about the game?

It was the only time Pitt won in the Rose Bowl. In Rose Bowl competition, Pitt is one and three.

Only a handful of schools have won more National Football Championships than the University of Pittsburgh. How many schools have more National Football Championships than Pitt?

Five. Notre Dame is first with 17. Pitt has 9.

Has the Pitt Panther football team ever gone a whole season with its opponents scoring zero points?

Yes. In 1910. That's right, 0 points for a whole season.

How many University of Pittsburgh football players have been named first team All-Americans?

68.

In the 15 seasons Jock Sutherland coached Pitt football, how often did Pitt shut out its opponents?

79 times, or 55 percent of the games.

How many Pitt football players went on to become head coaches in the National Football League?

Eleven. They are Luby DiMelio, Mike Ditka, Hal Hunter, Bill McPeak, Mike Nixon, John Michelosen, Joe Schmidt, Marty Schottenheimer, Jock Sutherland, Joe Walton, Dave Wannstedt.

Does Dan Marino hold the career passing yards record for the Pitt Panther football team?

No. Alex Van Pelt (1989-1992) is first with 11,267 career passing yards. Marino who played between 1979-82 is second with 8,597 career passing yards.

I n 1941, this local college powerhouse led the country in total defense, rushing defense and fewest points allowed per game (2.8 points). Name the school.

Duquesne University. Besides the low point total, Duquesne allowed 110.6 total yards and 56.0 rushing yards per game.

I n 1926, Carnegie Tech beat what team 19 to 0 in a game that some sports fans consider the most monumental upset in the history of college football?

Carnegie Tech beat Notre Dame at Forbes Field. Notre Dame coach Knute Rockne was so sure of a win that he didn't show up for the game, electing to scout Navy for a game to be played the following year!

H ow many All-Americans have played football at Carnegie Tech (now Carnegie Mellon University)?

Two. Defensive tackle Lloyd Yoder (1926) and quarterback Howard Harpster (1928). Harpster was the quarterback in 1926 when Tech beat Notre Dame 19 to 0.

H ow many Pitt Panthers' players and coaches are in the College Football Hall of Fame?

23. The last inductee was Mark May, who played at Pitt between 1977-1980. He was inducted into the College Hall of Fame in May 2005.

W hen is the last time a Duquesne University football team played in a major bowl game?

1936. Duquesne played in the Orange Bowl against Mississippi State. Duquesne won 13 to 12.

Washington & Jefferson set a NCAA Division III football record by scoring how many points in one quarter?

They scored 49 points in the first quarter against Emory & Henry on October 25, 2004. W & J (no surprise) won 76-28.

FOOTBALL: PRO

When is the only time in their history that the Steelers, in a single game, had a 400-yard passer, a 200-yard receiver, a 100-yard receiver and a 100-yard rusher? Hint: Tommy Maddox (473 yards passing); Plaxico Burress (253 yards receiving); Hines Ward (139 yards receiving); Amos Zereoue (123 yards rushing).

The 2002 overtime game against the Atlanta Falcons ended in a 34-all tie.

Who was the U.S.'s first pro football player?

William "Pudge" Heffelfinger. He played a professional football game in 1892 at a spot near Three Rivers Stadium. He's believed to be the first player to be paid to play the game.

How many years did the Pittsburgh Maulers play football?

The Maulers managed to play one season in the United States Football League during the spring of 1984. Their record was 3 and 15. They also lost about $6 million.

Which former all-pro NFL quarterback was also a quarterback for Saint Justine High School in Pittsburgh and also for a semi-pro team in Pittsburgh, the Bloomfield Moose?

John Unitas.

It is unlikely to happen today, but when did the Steelers have a first round draft pick from football powerhouse Duquesne University and who was he?

Mike Basrak, who was a center, was drafted in 1937.

How many quarterbacks have been chosen by the Steelers as first round draft picks?

Ted Marchibroda (1953), Lenny Dawson (1957), Terry Bradshaw (1970), Mark Malone (1980) and Ben Roethlisberger (2004).

What is the correct name for the three objects that make up the logo on the Pittsburgh Steelers' helmets?

They are known as hypocycloids. The logo was created by the U.S. Steel Corporation (now known as USX Corporation). The logo now belongs to the American Iron and Steel Institute, which gave the Steelers permission to use it. The Steelers had to petition the AISI to change "Steel" to "Steelers" on the logo.

Who has the Steelers' single-season sack record?

Mike Merriweather with 15 in 1987.

Franco Harris is the all-time leading Steeler rusher with how many yards?

11,950 career yards.

When Steeler Franco Harris made his Immaculate Reception in 1972 against the Oakland Raiders, who was the intended receiver?

Frenchy Fuqua.

How many footballs do the Pittsburgh Steelers use in a game?

About 36. According to the Pittsburgh Post-Gazette, *12 footballs are given to game officials in a sealed box before each game with the letter "k" marked on it. These balls are used just for kicking, and the use of the sealed box avoids tampering with the balls.*

Who were the passer and the receiver for the longest quarterback-to-quarterback pass play in Steeler history?

Terry Bradshaw threw a 90-yard pass to Mark Malone in 1981 against Seattle.

What is the longest run from scrimmage by an NFL quarterback?

Steeler Kordell Stewart's 80-yard run against the Carolina Panthers on December 22, 1996.

Which back has the record for most yards rushing against the Steelers in a single game?

The Jacksonville Jaguars' Fred Taylor with 234 yards in 30 attempts (2000). The previous record was held by O. J. Simpson of the Buffalo Bills with 227 yards in 1975.

In how many seasons did the Steelers have a 1,000 yard rusher as well as a 1,000 yard receiver?

Only twice. Franco Harris and John Stallworth in 1979; and Jerome Bettis and Yancey Thigpen in 1997.

Which Steeler receiver has the record for the most catches in a single game?

Courtney Hawkins with 14 against Tennessee in 1998.

In what year were the Steelers founded?

1933. The Steelers have the fifth-oldest franchise in the NFL. The team was originally named the Pittsburgh Pirates, but in 1940 the name was changed to the Steelers.

When was the last time a Steeler running back won the NFL rushing title?

1946.

Which Steelers have the records for most yards received in a single game and for a single season?

Single game: Plaxico Burress, 253 yards (2002 vs. Atlanta Falcons); season: Yancey Thigpen, 1,398 yards (1997).

What are the Steelers' records for fewest yards gained rushing and fewest yards gained passing in a single game?

Fewest yards rushing: 7 (1966 vs. Dallas); fewest yards passing: minus 16 (1965 vs. Saint Louis Cardinals).

Which Steelers have the longest punts and longest field goals?

Punt: Joe Geri, 82 yards (1949). Gary Anderson (1984) and Kris Brown (2001) have each kicked 55-yard field goals.

When was the last time a Steeler quarterback threw for more than 400 yards in a game?

2002. Tommy Maddox picked up 473 yards against the Atlanta Falcons. Bobby Lane, back in 1958, threw for 408 yards against the Chicago Bears.

Which Steeler has the record for the most interceptions in a single game?

Jack Butler with four against Washington in 1953.

Which Steeler is the career and the season leader in interceptions?

Mel Blount with 57 career interceptions and 11 season interceptions.

Which Steeler has the most career total yards from scrimmage? Who holds the season record for total yards from scrimmage?

Franco Harris has the most career total yards from scrimmage: 14,243. Barry Foster has the season record for total yards: 2,034.

What was the best year for Steelers' attendance at Three Rivers Stadium?

1996. They drew 466,944 fans.

What's the biggest crowd to see the Steelers play at Three Rivers Stadium?

61,545 on January 15, 1995 in a post season game against San Diego. The Steelers lost 17-13.

What is the name of the first player the Steelers ever drafted?

Bill Shakespeare was the first. He was chosen in 1936. He was a quarterback from Notre Dame. There is no information available about his writing talents.

Did the Steelers ever lose a game in overtime at Three Rivers Stadium?

No. They were 6-0 in overtime at Three Rivers Stadium.

How many Steelers (players, coaches, owners) are in the NFL Hall of Fame?

19.

What was the only year in which no Steeler was chosen for the Pro Bowl?

2000.

Which Steeler has played in the most Pro Bowls?

Joe Green appeared 10 times. Four others have appeared nine times.

Who is the only NFL player to score six different ways in his career?

Steeler Bill Dudley. He scored by rushing, returning a kickoff, returning a punt, recovering a fumble, intercepting a pass and receiving a pass. He wasn't called "Bullet Bill" for nothing.

What are the Steelers' records for the longest punt and kickoff returns?

Longest punt return: 90 yards by Brady Keys in 1964; longest kickoff return: 101 yards by Don McCall in 1969.

What is the Steelers' longest run from scrimmage?

97 yards by Bobby Gage in 1949 against the Chicago Bears, resulting in a touchdown.

Which opposing player has the two longest runs from scrimmage against the Steelers?

O. J. Simpson for 94 and 88 yards in 1972 and 1975. Both runs went for touchdowns.

Mike Webster has the Steelers' record for playing the most consecutive games with 177. How close did center Dermontti Dawson get to tying Webster's record?

Dawson played in 170 consecutive games.

How many different Steelers have rushed for more than a 1,000 yards in a season?

Six. John Henry Johnson, Franco Harris, Rocky Bleier, Barry Foster, Jerome Bettis, Willie Parker.

Which Steeler has the record for the longest run from scrimmage at the Three Rivers Stadium?

Sidney Thorton ran for 75 yards against the Baltimore Colts in 1979.

Who was the first Pittsburgh Steeler to rush for more than 1,000 yards in a single season?

John Henry Johnson who gained 1,141 yards in 1962.

Art Rooney knew a bargain when he saw it.
Courtesy Carnegie Library of Pittsburgh.

A rt Rooney bought the Pittsburgh Steelers in 1933. How much did he pay for the team?

A reported, but unconfirmed, $2,500.00. That would be $33,865 in today's dollars.

A committee from the Pro Football Hall of Fame has selected an all-90s NFL team. How many Steelers were chosen?

Center Dermontti Dawson was the only Steeler chosen for the first team. Linebacker Levon Kirkland was a second team pick. A few ex-Steelers were chosen for either the first or second team: Kevin Greene, Rod Woodson, Hardy Nickerson, Carnell Lake and Gary Anderson.

When and why did the Steelers become the Steagles?

Because of World War II, there was a manpower shortage when it came to football. For one year (1943), the Pittsburgh Steelers and the Philadelphia Eagles joined as one team. The team was 5-4-1.

Match these Pittsburgh Steelers' Super Bowlers with the numbers on their uniforms: (1) Joe Greene, (2) Andy Russell, (3) Ray Mansfield, (4) Roy Gerela, (5) Sam Davis and (A) 10, (B) 56, (C) 57, (D) 75, (E) 34.

1. D; 2. E; 3. B; 4. A; 5. C.

Name the 1983 Steeler first-round draft pick who never played a regular season game because he became a quadriplegic following an auto accident.

Gabriel "Gabe" Rivera.

Who were the front four Steelers who made up the Steel Curtain during Super Bowls IX and X?

Joe Greene, L. C. Greenwood, Ernie Holmes, Dwight White.

How many jersey numbers have the Pittsburgh Steelers retired?

One, number 70. It belonged to defensive tackle Ernie Stautner, who played from 1950-1963.

Which Steeler quarterback (he was on the roster only in 1957) ran for the vice presidency of the United States?

Jack Kemp. He ran in 1996 as Bob Dole's running mate.

Which Steeler has the most career sacks?

Jason Gildon with 77. He played between 1994 and 2003.

What's the largest crowd to watch a Steelers home game?

There were 64,975 fans in the stands to see the Steelers beat the Philadelphia Eagles 27-3 on November 7, 2004.

GOLF

Name two of the four golfers who have won the West Penn Open and the U.S. Open. Naming all four is the trivia equivalent of a hole in one.

Sam Parks, Lew Worsham, Ed Furgol, Arnold Palmer.

How many golf courses are there in Western Pennsylvania?

Nearly 160 public and private courses (9 or more holes only).

Where is the Oakmont Country Club?

Only about 3 percent of the club is in Oakmont Borough. The rest is in Plum Borough, including the clubhouse. The country club's tool house is in Oakmont, however.

Which pro golfers designed the Nevillewood, Treesdale and Diamond Run golf courses?

Nevillewood in Collier Township south of Pittsburgh was designed by Jack Nicklaus; Treesdale in northern Allegheny County/southern Butler County was designed by Arnold Palmer and Diamond Run (in the Sewickley Area) by Gary Player.

What is the only major golf tournament Arnold Palmer has not won?

The PGA Championship.

How much prize money has Latrobe's Arnold Palmer won throughout his pro golf career?

$5,492,245.

Who are the only golfers to win the Western Pennsylvania Amateur and the Western Pennsylvania Junior Amateur Golf Tournaments in the same year?

Arnold Palmer won both tournaments in 1947 at the age of 16, each without the presence of an army. Fred Brand Jr. did it in 1927.

What is Western Pennsylvania's toughest golf course?

It is a tie. The Pittsburgh Business Times *reports the toughest courses are the Nemacolin Woodlands Resort and Spa/Mystic Rock (Farmington), Southpointe Golf Club (Canonsburg), and Treesdale Golf and Country Club (Gibsonia). Laurel Valley Golf Club in Ligonier is close behind. The ratings are based on criteria set by the Western Pennsylvania Golf Association and the Keystone Public Golf Association.*

HOCKEY

When did the Pittsburgh Pirates play hockey?

The 1925-26 and 1929-30 seasons.

What was the name of the Pittsburgh hockey team that played in the American Hockey League intermittently in the 1930s, '40s, '50s and '60s? What building did that team play in and where was the building located?

The team was the Pittsburgh Hornets. They played at the Duquesne Gardens, which was located in Pittsburgh's Oakland section near Fifth Avenue and Craig Streets.

What was the score in the Penguins largest shutout in team history?

10-0. The Pens beat Tampa Bay on November 1, 1995.

Which Penguins goalie recorded the most shutouts in a single season?

Tom Barrasso with 7 in 1997-98.

Which Penguin goalie has the most shutouts?

Tom Barrasso with 21.

How long did it take for Mario Lemieux to score his first NHL goal?

It was first game, first shift, first shot and within 78 seconds he got his first goal. The year was 1984. After he came out of retirement in December 2000, he needed only 33 seconds into the game to get an assist on a goal by Jaromir Jagr.

Did Mario Lemieux ever score 200 points or more in a single season?

No. His highest point total was 199 during the 1988-89 season.

What are the most points ex-Penguin Jaromir Jagr scored during one regular season?

In the 1995-96 season, Jagr had 62 goals and 87 assists for 149 points.

Who was the first Penguin to appear in an NHL All-Star game?

Ken Schinkel, in the 1967-68 season.

Only twice in NHL history has a team come from behind 0-3 in a seven game series and gone on to win the series. It happened to the Penguins. Who victimized the Pens and when?

In the quarter-finals of the 1975 playoffs, the New York Islanders swept the last four games to take the series. The other 0-3 comeback: The Toronto Maple Leafs beat the Detroit Red Wings in the 1942 Stanley Cup finals.

In what season did the Penguins have their largest regular season attendance? How many fans came?

In 1993-94, 685,589 fans attended home games.

The Pittsburgh Penguins have the NHL record for the most consecutive victories. How many games in a row did the team win?

The Pens won 17 consecutive games in 1993.

What Penguin has the record for the best plus/minus season?

In 1992-93, Mario Lemieux was plus 55. Two players are tied for second-best plus/minus (season). Lowell MacDonald, 1971-72, and Petr Nedved, 1995-96, were plus 37.

W̲ho is the first Pittsburgh-area born player to play in the National Hockey League?

The Penguins' Ryan Malone, who joined the team in 2003.

W̲hat is the fastest hat trick scored against the Penguins?

The New York Islanders' Derek King embarrassed goalie Tom Barrasso with three goals within 78 seconds in October 15,1991 at Nassau Coliseum. The Pens still won 7-6.

W̲hat were the greatest number of goals scored against the Penguins by an opponent?

The Pens lost 12-0 to Montreal on February 22, 1979 at the Forum.

W̲hat is the fastest time the Penguins were able to score 5 goals? 4 goals?

The fastest 5 goals took 2:07 to score. That was in 1972 against Saint Louis. In 1998, the fastest 4 goals were scored against Saint Louis, too. The time was 1:39. The Pens won by a 4-3 score.

W̲ho is the first American-born player to score 500 goals in the NHL?

Joe Mullen. Mullen played with the Pens between 1990-1995 and 1996-1997. He is now a coach in the Pens' system.

W̲ho has played the most games as a Penguin?

Jean Pronovost played 753 games as a Penguin between 1968 and 1978.

Which promising Penguin rookie died in a car accident in May of 1970?

Michel Briere.

What is the most number of penalties handed out to a Penguin in a single game?

Russ Anderson was a bad boy nine times against Edmonton on January 19, 1980.

What is the Penguin record for most assists in a game?

Six. It was done five different times by three different players. Mario Lemieux (three times), Ron Stackhouse, and Greg Malone.

Which Penguin has the record for the most shots in a game?

Ron Stackhouse with 14 on April 3, 1976 against Washington.

How many times in his career did Mario Lemieux score five goals in one game?

Three.

Which Penguin goalie has the season record for the most saves at home? Away?

Denis Herron set both records during the 1977-78 season. He had 938 saves at home and 982 saves on the road. He also has the single-season save record (1,920) set that same season.

What are the most shots taken against the Penguins in a game at home and away?

Montreal took 55 shots against the Penguins on October 23, 1976 for the home record. Chicago took 62 shots against the Pens in 1989 for the away record.

What is the most shots the Penguins have ever taken in a home game? Away?

65 against Washington on March 15, 1975. On the road, the most shots by the Penguins in a game were against Toronto (1974) and Chicago (1979), both 49 shots.

Who holds the Penguin record for scoring a point in the most consecutive games?

Mario Lemieux scored at least one point in 46 consecutive games during 1989-1990 season.

Who has scored the most career points against the Pittsburgh Penguins?

Wayne Gretzky with 124 points.

Which three Penguins goalies have the best season goals against averages?

Tom Barrasso, 2.07 in 1997; Jean Sebastien Aubin, 2.22 in 1998-1999; Les Binkley, 2.86 in 1970; Hank Bassen, 2.86 in 1967.

What is the fastest the Penguins scored two goals? Three goals?

The Penguins scored two goals in six seconds twice, both in February, 1990. The fastest the Penguins scored three goals was November 22, 1972.

What is the fastest the Penguins ever scored a goal after the start of a game?

Six seconds, scored by Jean Pronovost on March 25, 1976 at Saint Louis. Penguins lost 5-2.

In his career, Mario Lemieux has scored the most goals against the New York Rangers (53). Against what team has he served the most penalty minutes?

The Washington Capitals. He spent 92 minutes in the box against the Capitals. For second place, he served 87 penalty minutes against the New Jersey Devils.

Which player has scored the most goals against the Pittsburgh Penguins?

Mike Gartner (New York, Washington, Minnesota) has 56 goals.

Which goalie has the most shutouts against the Pittsburgh Penguins?

Bernie Parent (Toronto, Philadelphia) has shut out the Pens 10 times.

Which goalie has the most wins against the Pittsburgh Penguins?

Rogie Vachon with 34 wins. He played with Montreal, LA, Detroit and Boston.

Who is the only woman in the Pittsburgh Penguins Hall of Fame?

Elaine Heufelder. For more than 35 years she has been a key assistant in the operation of the team's front office as well as in the operation of Mellon Arena.

What is the estimated value of the Pittsburgh Penguins franchise?

In December 2003, Forbes Magazine *said $114 million. A year earlier,* Forbes *put a value of $130 million on the Pens.*

In what season did the Penguins achieve their best percentage when playing short-handed?

In 1997-98, they successfully defended 86.4 percent of the short-handed situations in which they found themselves. In 1982-83, they had a team low percentage playing short-handed, defending successfully only 72.2 percent of the time.

In what season did the Penguins have their most success in scoring power play goals?

In 1981-82, they scored in 24.5 percent of their power play situations (99-404). They have had as low as a 6.7 percent rating.

What is the record for most power play goals for both teams in a game involving the Penguins?

The Pens and New Jersey each scored five power play goals on October 29, 1989 at the Mellon Arena.

On average, how many pucks are used during a Penguins' game?

Around 36, or 12 a period.

Who is the first European-trained player to ever win the scoring title in the National Hockey League?

Jaromir Jagr. He won the title with 70 points in the 1994–95 season while playing for the Pittsburgh Penguins.

What were the Penguin colors before they were black and gold?

Dark blue, light blue and white. In 1980, the colors were changed to black and gold.

Who was the last National Hockey League goalie to play every minute of every regular season game?

Former Penguin coach Ed Johnston. He played in all 70 games in the 1963-64 season for the Boston Bruins.

BAIT 'N BULLETS

How many deer were harvested in the Pittsburgh area in 2002 (the last year the state reported figures by county)?

County	Antlered Deer	Antlerless Deer
Allegheny	3,693	6,577
Beaver	1,591	4,397
Butler	3,311	7,703
Fayette	2,920	4,606
Washington	3,743	11,193
Westmoreland	4,091	9,409
Total	19,349	43,885

In 2004, how many black bears were harvested in Pittsburgh-area counties?

106. Five in Butler. Fifty-seven in Fayette. Fourty-four in Westmoreland.

What's the biggest catfish to be found in area water?

The flathead catfish.

What's the biggest fish caught in Pennsylvania waters?

A 54-pound, three-ounce muskellunge caught in 1924 in Conneaut Lake.

How big was the biggest fish ever caught in the Pittsburgh area?

The record belongs to Pittsburgher Seymore Albramovitz. In 1985, he caught a 43-pound, nine-ounce flathead catfish in the Allegheny River in Allegheny County.

How many people in the seven-county Pittsburgh region had fishing licenses as of the end of 2004?

159,285. By county, that is: Allegheny (64,036), Beaver (12,765), Butler (20,106), Fayette (16,588), Washington (13,201), Westmoreland (32,589). Allegheny County has the most licensed anglers of any county in the state.

In the six-county Pittsburgh region, how many boats were registered with the state as of the end of 2004?

64,528 boats. By county: Allegheny (27,100), Beaver (6,367), Butler (9,002), Fayette (4,208), Washington (6,843), Westmoreland (11,008).

AND ALL THAT OTHER STUFF . . .

Which Pittsburgh wrestler and former construction worker became the WWF Heavyweight Champion on May 17, 1973 by defeating Nature Boy Buddy Rogers?

Bruno Sammartino. Sammartino was born in Italy and came to the U.S. at the age of 15. He remained the champion for 14 years except for a period between 1971-73 when he lost and then regained the championship belt.

Where and when was the last heavyweight championship boxing match in Pittsburgh? Who fought? Who won?

On July 18, 1951, Arnold Raymond Cream knocked out Ezzard Charles in seven rounds at Forbes Field to become world heavyweight champion. Boxing fans will know Cream as Jersey Joe Walcott.

A family from the Lawrenceville section of Pittsburgh had five sons who loved to box. One of them turned pro in 1931, eventually becoming the welterweight champion in 1940, beating Henry Armstrong. He beat Armstrong in a 1941 rematch, but lost the crown in his next defense. Which Pittsburgher was the nation's short-lived welterweight champ?

Fritzie Zivic. Zivic was born in 1913 and died in 1984. His boxing record was 159 wins, 64 losses and 9 draws. He had 80 KOs.

Blind in one eye, this Pittsburgh-born boxer (he was known as the "Pittsburgh Windmill") was better than most fighters with two good eyes. He fought in three weight divisions: middleweight, light heavyweight, and heavyweight. He won the light heavyweight title in 1922 (beating Gene Tunney, the only loss Tunney ever had) and the middleweight title 1923. He fought between 1913 and 1926. He died in 1926 at the age of 30 following a minor operation on his nose after a traffic accident. Gene Tunney was one of the pallbearers. Name the "Pittsburgh Windmill".

Harry Greb.

What is the fastest mile ever officially recorded on the 5/8s mile track at Ladbroke at the Meadows?

For pacers, the record for a mile is 1:49.3 held by Riyadh (1996) and Timesarechanging, Georgie Pacific, and Santastics Pan (all 2004). The 2004 records were all the same race. For trotters, the time is 1:54.1, set by SJ's Caviar (2001), Yankee Douglas (2002), and Hopes Victory (2004).

Jersey Joe down for the count. Photo by James G. Klingensmith, 1951.
Courtesy of the Carnegie Library of Pittsburgh. © Pittsburgh Post-Gazette.

In what year was the most money bet on harness racing that took place at Ladbroke at the Meadows?

In 1994, $97 million was bet. The daily record was set on August 13, 1994 when $1.6 million was bet.

In November 2004, driver Dave Pallone from Waynesburg, PA won seven races at the Meadows, his home track. The seventh win was a milestone for Pallone, one reached by only three other drivers in harness racing history. What did Pallone accomplish?

Pallone, the Meadows' all-time leading driver, won his 10,000th race.

Who is the only known professional athlete in the United States to compete over eight decades?

Harness racing driver Del Miller. Miller won his first race in 1929, his last in 1991.

Over its 19-year existence, how many runners died while running the City of Pittsburgh Marathon?

Three.

Measured in gallons, what is Western Pennsylvania's biggest swimming pool and how long does it take to fill it?

The pool at Allegheny County's North Park holds 2.3 million gallons of water. The county fills the pool over five, twenty-four hour continuous flow days so as not to interrupt the flow of water to other park facilities. The pool could be filled in two days with the valves completely open.

"Dimple" and "pinball" seem like harmless words. When can they be deadly?

When rafters on Ohiopyle's lower Youghiogheny bang into Dimple Rock or Pinball Rock and overturn, with potentially lethal consequences. Seven boaters have died there since the park opened in 1970.

How difficult to handle are the white water rapids at Ohiopyle State Park in Fayette County?

At times, Ohiopyle's 14 rapids hit a class IV difficulty using an international scale devised by the American Whitewater Association. Class IV are "rapids with constricted passages that often require precise maneuvering in very turbulent waters."

What is the name of the 150-mile, motor-free, recreational trail that will eventually connect Pittsburgh with Cumberland, MD where it will link with the C&O Canal Trail into Washington, DC?

The Great Allegheny Passage. The trail is now open between McKeesport and Cumberland, MD.

Identify the sports of these long-gone Pittsburgh professional teams: (1) Gladiators, (2) Maulers, (3) Spirit, (4) Pipers, (5) Triangles.

(1) Indoor football, (2) U.S. Football League, (3) indoor soccer, (4) professional basketball, (5) indoor tennis.

When you think of Pittsburgh sports, what do the following names have in common? The Spirit, the Condors, the Maulers, the Rens, the Ironmen, the Pirahanas, the Miners, the Bulls, the Gladiators, the Phantoms, and the Stingers.

They are all pro-sport franchises that have failed in the Pittsburgh market.

Biker Lance Armstrong is a six-time Tour de France winner. How many times did he win the now defunct Pittsburgh Thrift Drug Classic?

Twice, once in 1993 and again in 1994.

Where can a skier find the highest ski slope in Western Pennsylvania?

The highest is Blue Knob with a vertical drop of 1,072 feet.

What Western Pennsylvania ski facility has the steepest ski slope?

It is the "Lower Wildcat" slope at Laurel Mountain Ski Area. "Lower Wildcat" is classified as "Double Black Diamond," making it suitable for advanced skiers only.

What Western Pennsylvania ski resort has the most runs and trails as well as the longest run?

Blue Knob has 34 runs and trails and its Mambo Valley is the longest run, about two miles long.

It has not reached the level of winter Olympics competition yet, but snow-shovel riding has a following in Western Pennsylvania. What Beaver County town hosts the world championship snow-shovel riding contest?

Old Economy Park in Economy Borough.

Which Pittsburgher is a member of the United States Table Tennis Association Hall of Fame?

Dan Seemiller. Seemiller graduated from Carrick High School in 1971. He is also a five-time national singles champion and an 11-time national doubles champion. Finally, he invented a new way to hold a racquet. It is known as the Seemiller Grip. Seemiller was coach of the U.S. Table Tennis Olympic Team (2004).

What are the course records—men's, women's and wheelchair divisions—for the City of Pittsburgh Marathon?

Men: 2:10:24 (1995); Women: 2:29:50 (1988); Men's Wheelchair: 1:30:17 (2003); Women's Wheelchair: 1:57:42 (1995).

How many University of Pittsburgh athletes have won Olympic gold medals?

Two. John Woodruff won the gold for the 800-meter run in 1936. Olympian Roger Kingdom won gold medals in 1984 and 1988 for the 110-meter high hurdles.

"Flipping out" is an ever-present hazard at the Annual Pinburgh Tournament. What happens there?

Pinburgh is a pinball tournament sponsored by the Professional Amateur Pinball Association (PAPA). PAPA's headquarters are in cyberspace but the tournaments are usually held in Pittsburgh. The tournament went international in September 2004.

GOVERNMENT AND POLITICS

Pittsburgh's first Hizzoner, Ebenezer Denny.
Courtesy of the Carnegie Library of Pittsburgh.

After President Woodrow Wilson helped make the world safe for democracy in World War I, he and his attorney general, A. Mitchell Palmer, decided to keep the United States safe from communism. On January 2, 1920 the United States Department of Justice raided Communist party offices throughout America. Over 2,000 persons were arrested. How many were arrested in Pittsburgh?

There were 22 arrests made while a meeting was in progress on the third floor of the Communist Party of America district head-quarters located at 1207 Fifth Avenue downtown. Russian litera-ture and party membership cards were confiscated. Another 16 arrests were made in Youngstown, Ohio. The Wilson campaign against communism became known as the "Red Scare."

The official Allegheny County Seal has a ship, plough, and sheaves of wheat. What do those three items symbolize?

The ship symbolizes commercial traffic. The plough symbolizes agriculture and mining activities. The sheaves of wheat represent the county's harvest, both agricultural and the result of human industry.

185

What percentage of real estate within the city of Pittsburgh is exempt from paying any real estate taxes?

About 35 percent.

The Allegheny County morgue was moved, all in one piece, to its present location in 1928. Where was its original location?

It was across the street at Forbes and Ross streets where the County Office Building now stands.

How many streetlights does the City of Pittsburgh own within the city?

About 40,000. The figure also includes lights that are attached to walls and are under bridges, for example.

Which former Pittsburgh Pirates' pitcher (1968-69) now serves as a Republican member of the U.S. Senate from Kentucky?

Jim Bunning.

Which unsuccessful Republican candidate for president of the United States was born in West Middlesex Borough, Mercer County in 1887?

Alf Landon who ran against Franklin Delano Roosevelt in 1936.

Who was secretary of war under Abraham Lincoln and where was he born?

Edwin Stanton was born in Steubenville, Ohio in 1814. He practiced law in Pittsburgh in the 1840s. He served as secretary of war from January, 1862 until the end of the Civil War in 1865.

How many cat permits are issued in Allegheny County each year?

This is a trick question. The answer is none; cats in Allegheny County do not have to have licenses.

Which famous secretary of the U.S. Department of Interior was born in Altoona?

He was Harold L. Ickes and he was born in 1874. He was secretary of the interior from 1933 to 1945 under Franklin Delano Roosevelt and Harry Truman. Ickes also served as head of the Public Works Administration from 1933 to 1939.

Which Pittsburgher was the only African American to serve as a speaker of the Pennsylvania House of Representatives?

K. Leroy Irvis. Irvis served as speaker at various times between 1977 and 1987.

Who was the first African American to ever serve on Pittsburgh City Council?

Paul F. Jones, who served 1954 to 1960, was the first in modern times. Lemuel Googins was elected to council in 1881.

Who is the first African American *female* to serve on Pittsburgh City Council?

Valerie McDonald. She took office in 1994 and served until 2001.

Who was the first African American elected to a row office in Allegheny County?

Valerie McDonald Roberts became the Allegheny County recorder of deeds in 2002 after election in 2001.

Which Pittsburgh mayor served the longest?

David L. Lawrence. He served from 1946 to 1958 when he left to become Pennsylvania's governor. Lawrence died in 1966.

If there is a vacancy in Pittsburgh's mayor's office, that vacancy is filled by the president of city council. Who is next in line on council to the president?

If the president of council is unable or unwilling to serve, the next mayor is chosen by a majority vote of all of the members of council. This "interim mayor" serves only until the next election.

How many of Pennsylvania's governors have been elected from Allegheny County?

Five. The forgettable Francis Rawn Shunk and William Alexis Stone in the 19th century and, in more modern times, there have been James Duff, David L. Lawrence and Dick Thornburgh.

Who is the only person from Westmoreland County elected governor of Pennsylvania?

John White Geary who served from 1867 to 1873. Geary was a Union officer during the Civil War.

What is the official name of the federal building at Liberty Avenue and Grant Street in downtown Pittsburgh?

The William S. Moorehead Building, dedicated in 1964. Moorehead was a U.S. Congressman from the City of Pittsburgh.

How many gallons of wastewater does Alcosan treat each day?

About 200 million gallons a day.

David L. Lawrence:
A Democrat with an elephant?
Courtesy of the Carnegie Library
of Pittsburgh.

The city of Pittsburgh's 175+ refuse workers and 46 trucks pick up how much refuse on an average day?

About 500 tons.

How many dog licenses were sold in Allegheny County in 2004?

About 103,000.

How many lawyers practice law in Allegheny County?

Close to 6,500.

Why are all the fire hydrants within the city of Pittsburgh painted either red, yellow or green?

The colors indicate the size of the main waterlines that feed the hydrants. That way, firefighters know how much water pressure is at a hydrant. For example, green indicates a 24-inch line.

How many marriages took place in Allegheny County in 2004?

There were 6,949 marriage licenses issued. However, 3,043 divorces were granted and 3,129 couples filed for divorce.

How much money did the 1/2 percent sales tax dedicated to Allegheny County's Regional Asset District produce in 2004?

$72.5 million. That's about $1.1 million less than the previous year.

For the year 2006, what are the largest allocations for the Allegheny County Regional Asset District? (RAD is funded by a 1/2 percent sales tax collected on sales traced to Allegheny County).

The largest allocations are (in millions): Carnegie Library of Pittsburgh, $16.4; Allegheny County Regional Parks, $14.9; Sports and Exhibition Authority (stadiums), $13.4; Allegheny County Library Association, $7.7; City of Pittsburgh Parks, $5.2; the Pittsburgh Zoo and PPG Aquarium, $3.1; the Carnegie Museums, $2.6; Sports and Exhibition Authority (Mellon Arena), $2.4; Phipps Conservatory and Gardens, $1.9; the National Aviary, $1.0; McKeesport's Renziehausen Park, $0.6.

What is the City of Pittsburgh's total long-term debt? That's total interest and principal.

At the beginning of 2005, it was $1.25 billion in long-term debt. That comes out to $3,731 for every man, woman and child in the city.

Who is the best judge in the Allegheny Court of Common Pleas?

Judge R. Stanton "Tony" Wettick. The results are from an Allegheny County Bar Association survey conducted in 2000. The lawyers were asked to grade 49 county judges on their impartiality, legal ability, diligence and temperament.

How many people served on juries in the Allegheny County Common Pleas Court System in 2004?

The county summoned 40,558 people. Only 18,911 served.

An Allegheny County flag, now on display at the Allegheny County Court House in downtown Pittsburgh, has been to a spot were few have ventured. Where?

Astronaut Jim Irwin, a native of the Beechview area of the City of Pittsburgh, took the flag to the moon with him in 1971 as part of Apollo 12.

What is special about Pittsburgh's Fraternal Order of Police (FOP) Lodge?

The Pittsburgh Fraternal Order of Police was started in 1915 and is the oldest in the country.

How many organizations are licensed to operate bingo games in Allegheny County?

The number fluctuates throughout the year, but around 490 is a good estimate. The organizations are allowed to hold no more than two games a week.

Allegheny County has a seven percent hotel/motel tax, which is added to each room rental. How much does the tax produce each year?

In 2004, it produced $17,029,095. About 40 percent of the money collected goes to the Pittsburgh Convention and Visitors Bureau to promote tourism.

How many people die prematurely each year in the Pittsburgh area because of polluted air?

An estimate is 1,216 people. The number comes from a non-profit environmental group, Natural Resources Defense Council, which rates nearly 240 urban areas on the quality of air. Don't feel too bad. The NRDC say 5,873 people die prematurely each year in Los Angeles because of poor air.

What is the highest number of cats and dogs you are allowed to keep in your home in the city of Pittsburgh?

No more than five cats and dogs in any combination.

How many Western Pennsylvania individuals and business organizations filed for bankruptcy in 2004?

20,523. In 1999, the figure was 11,730.

How many gallons of water does the Pittsburgh Water and Sewer Authority purify each day?

About 65 million gallons. Most of what is removed are microbial contaminants such as viruses and bacteria.

What is the most frequent complaint filed with the Pittsburgh Commission on Human Relations?

About 80 percent of the complaints filed deal with possible discrimination in employment. Second are complaints about discrimination in housing.

Who was the last Republican mayor of Pittsburgh? When did he last serve?

John S. Herron. He took office in 1933 and served until December 31, 1934.

When is the last time a Republican served in Pittsburgh City Council?

December 31, 1939, when Councilman Robert Garland and Charles Anderson had their terms expire. Garland was known as the "Father of Daylight Savings Time" because of his fight to turn the clocks ahead in the spring.

True or False. Within the city of Pittsburgh, there are about five times as many Democrats registered to vote as there are Republicans.

True.

In Allegheny County, what is the ratio between Democrats and Republicans in voter registration?

There are 2.12 Democrats to every Republican.

Who is the first woman to serve as Pennsylvania's lieutenant governor?

Catherine Baker Knoll, who was elected to the job in 2002, serving with Governor Ed Rendell.

Which independent-minded Pittsburgh mayoral campaign slogan was "Nobody's Boy"?

Pete Flaherty. He was elected mayor in 1969 as a Democrat. Flaherty was elected to two terms as mayor. He died in 2005.

How many parking meters are in the city of Pittsburgh?

8,118. There are 6,368 on-street meters and 1,750 in parking lots. All those meters brought $4.8 million to the city's Parking Authority in 2004.

How much money in sales tax did the state collect from the seven-county Pittsburgh region during fiscal year 2004?

$730,131,000. By county, that's Allegheny ($491.7), Beaver ($24.3), Butler ($49.1), Fayette ($28.4), Washington ($58.3), and Westmoreland ($109.0). (Figures are in millions.)

In dollars, what is the biggest lawsuit the City of Pittsburgh ever lost?

Sol Gross in July, 2000 received his last check from the city to settle a case. The total amount paid to Mr. Gross was $13,909,036.50. It seems the city built soccer fields on Gross' property without his approval. He sued and won. The property is in South Oakland near Panther Hollow in Schenley Park.

What is the total amount of debt Allegheny County is allowed by law to accumulate without voter approval?

Take the average amount of money Allegheny County has spent in the last three year's budgets prior to any new borrowing. Multiply that average amount by three for the maximum borrowing without voter okay.

How much money did people in the six-county Pittsburgh area *bet* on the state lottery during fiscal year 2004?

By county: Allegheny ($303.4), Beaver ($36.3), Butler ($30.0), Fayette ($32.8), Washington ($40.9), Westmoreland ($86.8) for total bets of $530.2. (Figures are in millions.)

How much money did people in the six-county Pittsburgh area *win* by playing the Pennsylvania lottery in 2004?

By county: Allegheny ($146.8), Beaver ($16.1), Butler ($15.1), Fayette ($16.4), Washington ($19.5), Westmoreland ($49.7) for total winnings of $263.6. (Figures are in millions.)

How much money in commissions did retailers in the six-county Pittsburgh area make by selling lottery tickets in fiscal year 2004?

By county: Allegheny ($14.8), Beaver ($2.5), Butler ($1.8), Fayette ($2.0), Washington ($1.9), Westmoreland ($4.1) for total commissions of $27.1. (Figures are in millions.)

How many video gambling machines are licensed to operate in the city of Pittsburgh?

The figure varies but in mid-2000 there were 378 poker machines and 734 casino-type machines. There also were 973 recreational video game machines licensed.

How many state lottery outlets are in the Pittsburgh area?

County	Instant	Online	Total
Allegheny	31	804	835
Beaver	2	109	111
Butler	8	95	103
Fayette	11	119	130
Washington	5	150	155
Westmoreland	20	261	281
Totals	77	1,538	1,615

How many Sister Cities does Pittsburgh have throughout the world? Extra credit for naming them!

Fifteen. They are: Saarbrucken, Germany (1956); Bilbao, Spain (1960); Zagreb, Croatia (1979); Sheffield, United Kingdom (1980); Wuhan, China (1982); San Isidro, Nicaragua (1987); Sofia, Bulgaria (1993); Saitama (formerly Omiya), Japan (1997); Matanzas, Cuba (1998); Fernando de la Mora, Paraguay (1999); Donets'k, Ukraine (1999); Skopje, Macedonia (2001); Ostrava, Czech Republic (2001); Presov, Slovakia (2002); and Karmiel, Israel (2006). The figures represent the year that each city signed a Sister Cities agreement.

During 2003, how many foreign citizens applied for and received their U.S. citizenship in the Pittsburgh area?

798.

Of the 798 people who became U.S. citizens in 2003 by applying through local U.S. district courts, from what five foreign countries did most of the people migrate?

India (105), China (71), Bosnia and Herzegovina (54), and the former Soviet Union and Vietnam, (44 each).

How many foreign countries maintain consuls in Pittsburgh?

Twelve. They are Austria, Belgium, Canada, Croatia, Czech Republic, France, Germany, Georgia, Italy, Slovak Republic, Switzerland, United Kingdom.

How much money is in the City of Pittsburgh's budget to remove graffiti?

About $250,000.

When did Pittsburgh incorporate as a city and who was the city's first mayor?

Ebenezer Denny was elected as the first mayor in 1816.

How many local government units—cities, boroughs, townships, school districts, and authorities—are in Allegheny County?

263.

How many volunteer fire departments are there in the six-county Pittsburgh region?

535. By county, that's Allegheny (213), Beaver (53), Butler (36), Fayette (52), Washington (53), Westmoreland (128).

How life-threatening is it to be either a police officer or firefighter in the City of Pittsburgh?

Since 1885, fifty-nine police officers have been killed in the line of duty. Over a nearly comparable period of time, anywhere from 125 to 150 firefighters have been killed. (In earlier years, accurate records were not always kept.)

What municipality in Pennsylvania was the first to introduce reverse "911" calls?

Baldwin Borough in Allegheny County. With reverse 911, the Baldwin Borough police can automatically send recorded messages to residents of the borough. The service started in the year 2000.

Why is the Pittsburgh Platform of 1885 an important event in the history of Judaism?

The Pittsburgh Platform articulated the most comprehensive philosophy of the Reform Movement in American Judaism.

In international relations, what is the significance of the Pittsburgh Agreement?

On May 30, 1918, Czechs and Slovaks agreed to form the country of Czechoslovakia. The signing took place at a Moose lodge located at Seventh and Penn in downtown Pittsburgh. A plaque in the office building now at that location commemorates the event.

If a house straddles the dividing line between two different municipalities, which municipality gets to collect the real estate taxes on the house?

The municipality in which the house's master bedroom is located collects the real estate taxes.

Which two municipalities are partially in Allegheny County and also in other counties?

McDonald is also in Washington County and Trafford lies partially in Westmoreland County.

One Allegheny County municipality owns and maintains 10,000 to 11,000 "street trees." Street trees are planted on sidewalks close to public thoroughfares. This municipality also has about 12,000 residences including condos, apartments and houses. What is the name of this municipality owning just about one tree for each residential unit within its borders?

The municipality of Mount Lebanon.

Is Ellwood City a city?

No. It's a borough. To make matters more confusing, Ellwood City, the borough, is in two different counties, Beaver and Lawrence.

Besides Pittsburgh, how many other municipalities in Pennsylvania have a spelling that ends in "burgh?"

None. Pittsburgh rocks!

WHO WE ARE AND HOW WE LIVE

Teutonia Männerchor was founded in 1854 in Allegheny City (now Pittsburgh's North Side) by German immigrants who wanted to pass their heritage on to future generations. This "singing society" is still going strong today. Over 25% of Allegheny County residents are of German ancestry. Courtesy of Teutonia Männerchor and Alpen Schuhplattler und Trachtenverein.

How large does the city of Pittsburgh's population grow every day because of people coming into the city to work?

According to the 2000 census, Pittsburgh has a net daytime increase of 138,191 people (182,030 enter the city and 43,839 leave). The municipalities of Penn Hills, Mount Lebanon, Ross and Shaler have the most people entering the city to work. Pittsburgh's daytime population grows by 41.3%, the fourth largest percentage increase of any city (Washington, DC is first). It's important to note that not included in the increase are college students coming to school, shoppers, patients at hospitals or doctor's offices, or visitors.

What percentage of the people presently living in the Pittsburgh area have lived in the same house for 30 years or more?

Allegheny	19.5
Beaver	23.3
Butler	14.8
Fayette	22.4
Washington	21.7
Westmoreland	22.6

According to RealSTATs, a local real estate information company, what are the most expensive housing sales in the City of Pittsburgh and Allegheny County (outside of Pittsburgh)?

In Pittsburgh it's a house at 77 Woodland Road East, which sold for $2,214,875 in 2004. Outside of Pittsburgh, a house on Pinkhouse Road (Sewickley Heights) sold for $2,400,000 in 2001.

Again, based on information supplied by RealSTATs, what two houses have the highest assessed values as determined by the Allegheny County assessors?

A house on Holyrood Road in Squirrel Hill has the highest assessed value in Pittsburgh: $1,747,200. Within Allegheny County there's a home in Bell Acres Borough (on Beech Ridge Road), which has an assessed value of $9,130,300. The highest assessed value for all property in Allegheny County is the Pittsburgh International Airport, which has an assessed value of $1,674,184,600.

What does RealSTATs say are the most expensive commercial real estate sales to take place in Pittsburgh and Allegheny County?

Within Pittsburgh, PPG Place sold for $185,586,420 in 1999 and South Hills Village Mall in Bethel Park/Upper Saint Clair sold for $97,103,902 in 1991.

Volunteers prepare Meals on Wheels in Avonworth. Courtesy of The Lutheran Service Society.

I n an average year, how many meals does the Lutheran Service Society of Western Pennsylvania's Meals on Wheels program distribute?

Meals on Wheels distributes about 1.2 million meals annually in Allegheny County. In the tri-state area, they pass out about 2.3 million meals a year.

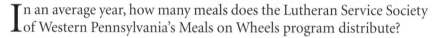

H ow many Alcoholics Anonymous groups are in the Greater Pittsburgh area?

About 560. They hold approximately 600 meetings a week.

H ow many births took place at Magee-Womens Hospital in 2005?

About 8,500. Since its start in 1911, Magee-Womens Hospital has delivered over 500,000 babies. It reached that plateau in December, 2005 with the delivery of a set of twins.

H ow many labor unions have their international headquarters in the Pittsburgh area?

Two: The United Steelworkers of America and the United Electrical Radio and Machine Workers of America.

What percentage of the people working in the Pittsburgh area work for either local, state or federal government?

By county: Allegheny (10.0%), Beaver (9.0%), Butler (9.7%), Fayette (10.5%), Washington (9.9%), Westmoreland (9.7%).

What percentage of the people in the Pittsburgh area are self-employed?

By county: Allegheny (5.2%), Beaver (5.3%), Butler (5.7%), Fayette (6.1%), Washington (5.9%), Westmoreland (5.8%).

According to the 2000 U. S. Census, how large was the drop in Pittsburgh's population between April 1, 1990 and April 1, 2000?

Pittsburgh's population went from 369,879 in 1990 to 334,563 in 2000. That's a loss of 35,316 people or 9.5%. The Pittsburgh metropolitan area lost 36,116 people (-1.5%) between April 1, 1990 and April 1, 2000. Of the 42 largest urban areas in the U.S., Pittsburgh was the only one to lose people during that period. The figures: 1990 (2,394,811) and 2000 (2,358,695). The Pittsburgh area is the nation's 22nd largest metropolitan area.

How many hospitals and hospital beds are in the Pittsburgh area?

Hospitals	Number	Beds
Allegheny	32	7,903
Beaver	3	497
Butler	3	269
Fayette	3	391
Washington	3	582
Westmoreland	7	1,223
Total	51	10,865

How clean is the air Pittsburghers breathe?

According to the Environmental Protection Agency's Air Quality Index (AQI), in 2003 Pittsburgh had 156 "good" air days and 209 days which were not classified as good. The air quality for those 209 days, in turn, was broken down as "moderate" (172 days), "unhealthy for sensitive groups" (people with breathing difficulties, 28 days), and "unhealthy" (9 days). The AQI measures the amount of particulate matter (small particles), ozone, sulfur dioxide and carbon dioxide in the air. The AQI ranges go from good to very unhealthy.

What percentage of the housing units in the Pittsburgh area were built before 1940 or after 1995?

County	Before 1940	After 1995
Allegheny	32.2	2.7
Beaver	28.5	3.7
Butler	20.1	11.6
Fayette	37.1	4.4
Washington	32.2	5.4
Westmoreland	26.5	4.9

What percentage of people living in the Pittsburgh area own their own home?

County	Owners	%	Renters	%	Total
Allegheny	360,036	67.0	177,114	32.9	537,150
Beaver	54,367	74.9	18,209	25.1	72,576
Butler	51,285	77.8	14,577	22.1	65,802
Fayette	43,876	73.2	16,093	26.8	59,969
Washington	62,561	77.1	18,569	22.9	81,130
Westmoreland	116,849	77.9	32,964	22.0	149,813

How do people in the Pittsburgh area heat their houses? (by percent)

County	Gas	Electric	Fuel Oil	Coal	Wood
Allegheny	88.3	8.5	1.5	0.0	0.1
Beaver	72.0	8.4	15.1	0.1	0.9
Butler	66.4	12.4	14.6	0.2	1.6
Fayette	44.5	12.5	35.1	2.1	1.6
Washington	67.7	15.2	13.4	0.2	1.4
Westmoreland	65.4	11.1	19.6	0.4	1.0

What percentage of the families in the Pittsburgh area have incomes in excess of $100,000 a year?

County	# of households	Percent of all households
Allegheny	48,443	14.5
Beaver	4,046	8.0
Butler	6,273	13.3
Fayette	2,282	5.5
Washington	6,224	11.0
Westmoreland	10,734	10.2

What percentage of the families in the Pittsburgh area have incomes of less than $10,000 a year?

County	# of households	Percent of all households
Allegheny	18,676	5.6%
Beaver	2,538	5.0
Butler	1,887	4.0
Fayette	3,903	9.4
Washington	2,460	4.4
Westmoreland	4,315	4.1

What percentage of the Pittsburgh area population is African American or Hispanic?

County	African American	Hispanic
Allegheny	12.1%	0.9
Beaver	5.9	0.7
Butler	0.8	0.6
Fayette	3.5	0.4
Washington	3.2	0.6
Westmoreland	2.0	0.5

To what three ancestries do most Pittsburgh area people trace their roots?

County	Country	# of people	% of County Population
Allegheny	German	330,625	25.8
	Irish	235,697	18.4
	Italian	194,227	15.2
Beaver	German	50,326	27.7
	Italian	30,216	16.7
	Irish	29,025	16.0
Butler	German	63,441	36.4
	Irish	30,988	17.8
	Italian	18,216	10.5
Fayette	German	30,815	20.7
	Irish	21,427	14.4
	Italian	17,022	11.5
Washington	German	46,011	22.7
	Italian	33,736	16.6
	Irish	31,993	15.8
Westmoreland	German	103,626	28.0
	Italian	64,900	17.5
	Irish	54,648	14.8

W hat languages other than English are most spoken in the greater Pittsburgh area?

County	Foreign languages most spoken	Number of speakers
Allegheny	Spanish	15,708
	Italian	10,494
	German	6,256
	(Seven people in Allegheny County speak Navajo)	
Beaver	Spanish	1,860
	Italian	1,652
	German	629
	Greek	596
Butler	Spanish	1,545
	German	799
	French	578
Fayette	Spanish	1,287
	Italian	578
	Polish	433
Washington	Spanish	1,689
	Italian	1,002
	German	917
Westmoreland	Spanish	3,503
	Italian	2,092
	French	1,297
	German	1,259

H_ow many Native Americans live in Allegheny County and the surrounding area?

County	Number of Native Americans
Allegheny	1,593
Beaver	190
Butler	149
Fayette	168
Washington	175
Westmoreland	327
Total:	2,602

W_hat percentage of households in the Pittsburgh area do not have telephones?

County	Percent without a telephone
Allegheny	0.9
Beaver	1.2
Butler	1.0
Fayette	1.7
Washington	0.9
Westmoreland	0.8

W_hat percentage of the households in the Pittsburgh area have no vehicles available? What percentage have three or more?

County	Percent no vehicle	Percent three or more
Allegheny	16.2	10.0
Beaver	9.4	16.1
Butler	5.7	19.2
Fayette	11.5	17.1
Washington	9.5	16.7
Westmoreland	8.4	16.6

How many national fraternal insurance groups are headquartered in the Pittsburgh area? Name them.

Seven: Polish Falcons, Italian Sons & Daughters of America, Croatian Fraternal Union, Slovene National Benefit Society, National Slovak Society, Serb National Federation, William Penn Association (Hungarian).

What percentage of the people living in the Pittsburgh area use public transit between work and home?

County	% public transit
Allegheny	10.5%
Beaver	1.2%
Butler	0.4%
Fayette	0.4%
Washington	1.3%
Westmoreland	0.9%

What is the average commute time in minutes for Pittsburgh area workers?

County	In minutes
Allegheny	25.3
Beaver	24.5
Butler	25.3
Fayette	26.5
Washington	25.6
Westmoreland	25.4

Hﾠow do people in the Pittsburgh area go to work each day?

County	Drive alone	Carpool	Public transit	Walk	Other	Work-at-Home
Allegheny	72.1	10.0	10.5	4.1	0.7	2.5
Beaver	83.6	9.7	1.2	2.9	0.7	1.9
Butler	84.9	8.3	0.4	2.8	0.5	3.1
Fayette	83.1	11.6	0.4	2.5	0.5	2.0
Washington	82.5	9.9	1.3	3.2	0.6	2.5
Westmoreland	84.7	8.7	0.9	2.9	0.5	2.2

Wﾠhat percentage of the people in the Pittsburgh area (25 years or over) have college or graduate degrees?

By county: Allegheny (28.3%), Beaver (15.8%), Butler (23.5%), Fayette (11.5%), Washington (18.8%), Westmoreland (20.2%).

Hﾠow many people living in Allegheny County have doctorate degrees?

11,909. That's 1.3% of the total population. Males have 8,341 doctorates, females 3,568.

Wﾠhat percentage of the people in the Pittsburgh area (25 years or older) have not graduated from high school?

By county: Allegheny (13.7%), Beaver (16.4%), Butler (13.2%), Fayette (24.0%), Washington (17.4%), Westmoreland (14.4%).

Wﾠhat percentage of the Pittsburgh area population is under five years of age?

By county: Allegheny (5.5%), Beaver (5.4%), Butler (6.4%), Fayette (5.7%), Washington (5.5%), Westmoreland (5.2%). The national average is 6.8%.

What percentage of the Pittsburgh area population is over 65?

By county, Allegheny (17.8%), Beaver (18.4%), Butler (14.3%), Fayette (18.1%), Washington (17.9%), Westmoreland (18.3%). The national average is 12.4%

What local municipalities have the highest per capita incomes?

County	Town	Income
Allegheny	Fox Chapel	$80,610
Beaver	Homewood Borough	$34,486
Butler	Adams Twp.	$39,204
Fayette	South Union Twp.	$19,905
Washington	Green Hills Borough	$124,279
Westmoreland	Murrysville	$32,017

What is the highest Pittsburgh's population ever reached?

In 1950, the number was 676,806. The 2000 figure is 369,879.

What percentage of houses in the area are worth less than $50,000 or more than $300,000?

County	% less than $50,000	% more than $300,000
Allegheny	19.5%	3.2%
Beaver	18.1%	0.7%
Butler	6.4%	3.7%
Fayette	34.1%	1.0%
Washington	19.2%	3.5%
Westmoreland	13.4%	2.4%

There are 367 housing units in Allegheny County worth more than $1 million.

What is the average value of single-family, owner-occupied houses in the area?

County	Average value
Allegheny	$84,200
Beaver	$85,000
Butler	$114,100
Fayette	$63,900
Washington	$87,500
Westmoreland	$90,600

The U.S. average is $119,600.

What percentage of the population in area counties have fluoridated water?

County	Percent of population who have fluoridated water
Allegheny	93%
Beaver	26%
Butler	2%
Fayette	57%
Greene	82%
Washington	22%
Westmoreland	14%

What Pittsburgh-based club makes it possible for you to play chess with up to 25,000 different people without leaving home?

The Internet Chess Club was started by CMU computer science professor Danny Sleator. Its web site is www.chessclub.com and it costs $48 a year for membership. The Internet Chess Club has 25,000 members worldwide, and on any given day it has 10,000 chess matches going on in cyberspace. Throughout the world, there are about 300 grandmasters. About 100 of them play regularly with the Internet Chess Club. Want to test your skills?

How many people were murdered in Allegheny County in 2004? What year has the record for most homicides?

83. The record year was 1918 when 145 homicides occurred.

What local Internet service provider (ISP) has the most dial-up subscribers?

Nauticom Internet Service with 29,000 customers.

How many calls came into the City of Pittsburgh's 911 emergency phone number in 2004?

Slightly over 525,000. Starting in 2005, the city's 911 service became part of Allegheny County's emergency system.

How many calls did the Women's Center and Shelter of Greater Pittsburgh receive between 2003 and 2004 from people seeking help with a domestic violence crisis?

8,795.

The Pittsburgh Poison Center gets 128,000 incoming calls a year from the general public and medical professionals. How many of those calls are actual emergencies? The center answers calls for the western half of Pennsylvania.

About 67,000. About 6,000 are calls about animals. There are 53,000 calls about possible human poisonings. The main causes of poisoning in the home are medicines, cleaning products, cosmetics and plants.

How many people served time in the Allegheny County jail in 2004?

27,219.

What was the most money the United Way of Southwestern Pennsylvania raised in a single year?

In 1999, the United Way set a record: $39,123,043. Since 1955, nearly $1.2 billion has been raised.

What county in Pennsylvania has the most Penn State alumni living in it?

There are slightly over 22,000 Penn State alumni living in Allegheny County. No other county beats that figure. Over one-quarter of a million Penn State alumni live in Pennsylvania. Almost 442,000 live throughout the U.S.

How many people have permits to carry handguns in Allegheny County?

Slightly over 52,000. A license is valid for five years. There were 10,200 permits issued in 2004.

What percentage of Allegheny County residents have a firearm of any type in their home?

21 percent.

How polluted is the Pittsburgh area's air compared to other cities?

A nonprofit environmental group, Natural Resources Defense Council, rates nearly 240 urban areas on the quality of air. The Pittsburgh area comes out 28th worst with 54 deaths per 100,000 population attributable to particulate air pollution. In 2000, Pittsburgh ranked 48th. Without indexing, Pittsburgh is the 8th worst in the country with an actual 1,216 deaths a year attributed to air pollution.

The Make-A-Wish Foundation of Western Pennsylvania grants wishes to children facing a life-threatening illness. When did Make-A-Wish make its first wish and what was it?

In May 1983, Make-A-Wish flew Bryan McClinton to Texas to visit his uncle because the uncle gave Bryan the best piggy-back ride. From 1983 to mid 2005, Make-A-Wish has granted nearly 7,000 wishes.

How many Mr. Yuk stickers have been distributed throughout the world by the Pittsburgh Poison Control Center?

Over 900 million stickers.

How many members does the Pittsburgh Herpetological Society have?

About 200. The members have about 20,000 animals in their private collections. The youngest member in mid 2000 was only four weeks old. The animals (or "herpes" in society lingo) include snakes, lizards, frogs, toads, turtles and salamanders.

What are the first and last entries in the 2006 Verizon Greater Pittsburgh *White Pages*?

A Aabco is first and Zyzak, Theodore is last (Theodore lives in Collier Township).

Since Allegheny County started to record the totals in 1981, how many cases of AIDS have been reported in the county?

As of December 31, 2004 there have been 2,369 cases of AIDS reported. The figures do not cover people with HIV infections. HIV infections are not reported in Pennsylvania, only cases of AIDS.

The Pittsburgh-based Carnegie Hero Fund Commission awards Carnegie medals. What is the origin of the Commission and the awarding of the medals?

On January 25, 1904, a massive explosion killed 179 coal miners in a mine near Springdale, Pennsylvania. Two additional miners died during unsuccessful rescue attempts. In the aftermath, Andrew Carnegie started the fund to honor a civilian "who knowingly risks his or her own life to an extraordinary degree while saving or attempting to save the life of another person." Over its lifetime, the fund has awarded 8,902 medals and $27.7 million in grants throughout the U.S. and Canada.

What were the ages of the youngest and oldest females to give birth in 2002 in Allegheny County?

The youngest was 12 years old and the oldest was 49 years. Two females in each of the age groups gave birth.

What were the weights of the lightest and heaviest babies born in Allegheny County in 2002?

The lightest was 160 grams or 6 ounces. (The baby died shortly after birth). The heaviest was 5,675 grams or 12.5 pounds.

How old were the oldest people to die in Allegheny County in 2002?

One man died at 106. One woman died at 108.

How many people in 2004 were adopted in Allegheny County?

214. This number is down greatly from 1995 when 481 people were adopted. Five of the adoptees were adults: 18 and over.

How many boxes of cookies do the Girl Scouts of Southwestern Pennsylvania sell each year during their early year drive?

In 2005, the Southwestern Pennsylvania Scouts sold 1,537,776 boxes of cookies. The most popular variety is Tagalongs (peanut butter and chocolate).

In 2004, how many arrests did the City of Pittsburgh police make for driving under the influence?

816. A dramatic drop from 1999, when there were 1,880 arrests for DUIs.

In 2004, how many pieces of real estate, residential and commercial, exchanged hands in Allegheny County?

44,765. The figure includes private sales, sheriff sales, and transfers to relatives, among others.

How frequently do cremations take place in Allegheny County?

In 2005, the coroner's office estimated that there would be between 4,800 and 5,000 cremations. The cremation trend is definitely up: 1993 (1,941), 1999 (3,177).

What is the estimated number of homeless people in Allegheny County?

There has been an average of 2,200 homeless people in Allegheny County at any time over the past few years.

How many students attend the four area community colleges in Allegheny, Beaver, Butler and Westmoreland Counties?

About 28,000 full-time equivalent students.

Who are the richest people in Pittsburgh?

According to the March 27, 2006 issue of Forbes *magazine the richest are: Henry Hillman ($2.7 billion), Maggie Hardy Magerko ($2.0 billion), and Richard Mellon Scaife ($1.2 billion). Among the 793 billionaires, Hillman is ranked #258 and Magerko #382. At $1.2 billion, Mr. Scaife is ranked "only" #645.*

How many handguns were sold to area residents in 2003?

A total of 28,938. By county: Allegheny (12,814), Beaver (2,758), Butler (3,498), Fayette (3,635), Washington (4,393), Westmoreland (1,840).

How many suicides were reported in Allegheny County in 2004?

150.

How many patients arrive at Pittsburgh hospitals by emergency helicopters in an average year?

Somewhere between 10,500 and 11,500 patients. Life Flight delivers between 2,000 and 3,000; Stat One about 8,500.

It is not unusual to deposit checks or money at a bank, but what gets deposited at the Pittsburgh Cryobank?

Sperm to establish pregnancy in the future. The most common reasons for sperm cryopreservation is to maintain fertility before undergoing radiation therapy or perhaps a prostate operation.

How many calls does Duquesne Light receive for the time and temperature each day?

An average of 30,000 a day or 10,950,000 calls a year. The number to call is 412-391-4500.

Over the past few years how many people, on average, have gone through the Allegheny County Court system on DUI charges each year?

Nearly 4,400.

How many "protection from abuse" orders did the Allegheny County courts issue over the past few years?

An average of about 3,000 a year.

From what source do the overwhelming majority of residents within the city of Pittsburgh get their water?

Over 80 percent of the residents get water from the Allegheny River. The rest (mostly living in the southern part of the city) draw water from the Monongahela River. The Pittsburgh Water and Sewer Authority supplies the city's northern part (70 million gallons a day) and a private company handles the southern part.

Using accidental drug overdose deaths as a criterion, are more people in Allegheny County saying "no" to drugs?

No. In fact, drug-related deaths increased each year from 2000 (101 deaths) to 2004 (229).

When was Pittsburgh the typhoid capital of the world?

Between 1873 and 1907, during a worldwide epidemic, Pittsburgh had well over 100 deaths per 100,000 residents. The average for other northern cities was only 35 deaths per 100,000 people. Typhoid is spread through food and water contaminated with feces or urine. At the time of the epidemic, local residents drew water from the Allegheny and Monongahela rivers and dumped untreated sewage into the rivers as well. Communities upriver from Pittsburgh did the same.

What do Allegheny County adults say is their biggest health problem?

28 percent say it's arthritis/rheumatism. Back or neck problems are next at 14 percent.

How monogamous are Allegheny County adults?

64 percent say they have had sex with only one partner over a yearly period. Another 19 percent report having no sex.

What percent of adults in Allegheny County smoke?

27 percent (adults 18+). More males (29 percent) than females (25 percent) smoke. High school graduates are almost twice as likely to smoke than college graduates.

What percent of Allegheny County adults drink alcoholic beverages?

34 percent. The Allegheny County Health Department, which researched the question, defines drinking as having five or more alcoholic drinks within a 30-day period.

What three facilities in Allegheny County release the most pollutants into the air (2002 figures)?

Facility and location	Tons of emissions per year
Orion Power Midwest, Cheswick	48,311
U.S. Steel, Clairton	12,265
U.S. Steel, North Braddock	3,426

How prevalent are mobile homes in the Pittsburgh area? (2002 figures)

County	# of mobile homes	Mobile homes as percent of total housing
Allegheny	4,401	0.8%
Armstrong	3,948	12.2%
Beaver	4,382	5.6%
Butler	8,760	12.5%
Washington	6,161	7.1%
Westmoreland	12,282	7.6%

Business in the 'Burgh

The "stacks" at Homestead Works, then and now ... Courtesy of the Rivers of Steel National Heritage Area, Steel Industry Heritage Corporation.

Which Pitt football player came up with the idea for a Nerf football?

Fred Cox, a 1962 Pitt graduate, played for the Minnesota Vikings for 15 years as a kicker. He and a friend thought of the material used to make the Nerf football. Since the ball came out in 1972, over 50 million have been sold.

Of the 30 teams in Major League Baseball, the Pirates rank 24th in market value. What market value in dollars does *Forbes* magazine assign to the franchise?

In April, 2006, Forbes *placed a $250 million value on the Pirates.* Forbes *valued the New York Yankees at $1,026 billion (#1). The Tampa Bay Devil Rays were 30th at $209 million.*

Who was Pittsburgh's first millionaire?

John N. Ingham, in his book Making Iron and Steel *says it was perhaps Curtis G. Hussey. Hussey was born in York, PA and started his professional career as a physician. He left his practice to open a general store in Western Pennsylvania where he also began dealing in pork. Eventually, he invested in a copper mine in the Lake Superior region and became a copper manufacturer. Ingham claims that Hussey was "perhaps" a millionaire by the time of the Civil War.*

Nationally, where does the Pittsburgh area rank when it comes to the number of privately-run businesses that are at least 50 percent owned by women?

The Center for Women's Business Research put Pittsburgh at 32 out of the top 50 metropolitan areas. The rankings are based on the number of firms, employment, and sales. The Pittsburgh area has 67,505 private firms that are 50% or more owned by women. Those firms employ 138,000 people and have sales of $15 billion.

No one beats Wal-Mart when it comes to supermarket sales volume ($95 billion a year at 1,243 stores). How does Giant Eagle compare?

Giant Eagle, with 213 stores, has sales of $4.4 billion. It ranks 24th nationally to Wal-Mart's number 1. Supermarket sales nationally are $682 billion.

Which of these cities has the lowest percentage of its private sector work force belonging to a union: Los Angeles, Seattle, San Francisco, or Pittsburgh?

It's Pittsburgh, with 9.5% of its private work force unionized. The percentages for the other cities: Los Angeles (9.6%); San Francisco (11.0%); and Seattle (13.2%). Detroit, at 19.3%, has the country's highest rate of private sector unionization.

About 325,000 people work within the city of Pittsburgh. How many of those workers also live in the city?

Approximately 155,000 people (47.7%) live and work inside the city of Pittsburgh. Around 170,000 (52.3%) work in the city but live somewhere else.

In the late 1880s the Mellon family and the Pittsburgh Reduction Company financed Charles Martin Hall's discovery. Hall found a way to extract a very common metal from earth's crust so that the metal could have wide commercial application. What is the metal?

Aluminum. The Pittsburgh Reduction Company later became Alcoa.

What do World War II airplanes, PPG Industries (Pittsburgh Plate Glass Company until 1965), eye glasses and something called CR-39 have in common?

During World War II the Allies faced a shortage of natural raw materials. PPG and other companies began experimenting with ways to make thermoplastic materials. A PPG subsidiary in Ohio, the Columbia Southern Chemical Company, after various unsuccessful attempts, developed a product on its 39th try: Columbia Resins 39. The first commercial use of CR-39 was to combine it with fiberglass to make a new fuel tank for B-17 bombers. Replacing the conventional fuel tank reduced a plane's weight and extended a plane's range. Next, CR-39 went into tubes inside fuel lines that led into a flight engineer's compartment, providing a gauge to read the fuel flow to a plane's engines. The older glass tubes broke easily and spewed gas into the cockpit. After the war, PPG ended up with a railroad tank car full of CR-39 resin (38,000 pounds). The optical industry showed interest in the product and before long plastic eyeglasses using CR-39 came into use. By 1975 more than 90% of PPG's CR-39 sales went to the optical business. Today plastic lenses make up the vast majority of the U.S. market.

What local steel company engineered, fabricated and erected the Jefferson Memorial Arch in Saint Louis, Missouri?

Pitt-DesMoines Inc. PDM started business in 1892. Its corporate headquarters are on Neville Island. The arch was completed in 1965, and towers 630 feet above the Saint Louis waterfront. The arch is the tallest monument in the United States.

In 1989, Chevron bought Gulf Oil, paying cash for the purchase. How much did Chevron pay? How much profit did Gulf shareholders make in the transaction?

Chevron paid $13.2 billion or $80 a share for Gulf. At the start of the takeover, Gulf's stock was selling for about $41 a share. The shareholders made a profit of $6.5 billion.

In the early to mid 1880s, Bakewell's, located in Pittsburgh, had a reputation for producing the finest objects in its field. Bakewell's was the first American company to supply its products to the White House. What was Bakewell's industry?

Bakewell's was one of America's finest glassmakers.

In 1900, New York City's first electric billboard carried an ad for what Pittsburgh-based company?

H.J. Heinz. The 1,200 lightbulb sign was at 23rd Street and Fifth Avenue.

The G. C. Murphy Variety Store chain started in McKeesport in 1906. What name goes with the "G" in G. C. Murphy?

It is George C. Murphy. The chain's founder, however, sold out early to two other businessmen.

The United Kingdom's Beazer PLC took over what long-time Pittsburgh corporation for $1.8 billion in 1988?

Koppers. The Koppers headquarters still stands at Seventh Avenue and Grant Street in an art deco skyscraper built in 1928.

What Golden Triangle office building has the most usable square feet?

The USX Tower with 2,336,272 square feet.

Where is the world's oldest, still-functioning oil field?

Titusville, PA.

In square feet, what is Western Pennsylvania's biggest shopping center?

The Waterfront has 1.5 million square feet.

Century III Mall is built on a U.S. Steel slag heap. How much slag had to be removed to prepare the site for construction of the mall?

An estimated 70 million tons of slag were dropped at the site between 1913 and 1970. The material was 200 feet high and could cover 130 city blocks.

Until recently, what percentage of the lubricating and motor oils produced in the U.S. came from Western Pennsylvania?

Twenty-five percent of the lubricating oil, and an even higher percentage of the motor oil's market. Pennsylvania oil is pure and does not require complicated refining. It is made of molecules that resist change under heat and pressure.

What Pittsburgh company is the largest specialty steel producer in the U.S.?

It's Allegheny Technologies. The company produces about one-quarter of all the specialty steel in the country. In 2003, a little less than 2 million tons of specialty steel were shipped in the U.S., and Allegheny Technologies was responsible for about 475,000 tons of that total.

How many pieces of mail (letters, cards, magazines, some packages) does the U.S. Post Office's Pittsburgh district headquarters handle each day?

The local post office processes about 1.6 million letters, cards, magazines, and some packages each day. Historically, the busiest day of the year is the Monday before Christmas, when it is not unusual to process over three million cards and letters.

How many pieces of mail does the Pittsburgh area office of the U.S. Postal Service forward each day to people who have changed addresses?

About 69,000 pieces of mail get forwarded daily to people who have moved.

How many delivery points does the U.S. Postal Service Pittsburgh headquarters service each day?

About one million.

Where was GNC's first store located and what was the store's original name?

The first store opened on February 1, 1951 on Wood Street in downtown Pittsburgh. The company name at the time was Lack-zoom.

W hat area labor union is the biggest, based on annual receipts?

The Pittsburgh Business Times *(based on 2003 receipts) ranks the Electrical Workers IBEW, AFL-CIO Local 5, as the largest with receipts of $13.5 million. The next four: Operating Engineers, AFL-CIO Local 66 ($11.3 million); Boilermakers AFL-CIO Local 154 ($7.9 million); Food and Commercial Workers AFL-CIO Local 23 ($5.7 million); Ironworkers, AFL-CIO Local 3 ($3.7 million).*

W hat Pittsburgh company invented the magnetic ink used to print stripes on Universal Product Codes (UPCs)?

Matthews International in the South Hills. Matthews and one of its employees, Lawrence M. Flamberg, are credited with the invention. Flamberg died in 1997.

P resumably, anyone who knows what *resorcinol* is would know that this company's plant in Petrolia, Butler County is the world's largest *resorcinol* plant. What's the company? Better yet, what is *resorcinol*?

The company is Indspec Chemical Corporation. Resorcinol is a chemical block that enhances the performance of rubber and plastic. It protects plastic from exposure to sunlight. Resorcinol also makes computer casings and indoor piping more fire retardant.

W hat foreign-owned corporation employs the most people in the Pittsburgh area?

Westinghouse Electric Company employs 3,000 people locally. The long-time Pittsburgh-based company was sold to a consortium led by British Nuclear Fuels, PLC in 1999. BNFL in turn accepted an offer from Toshiba in 2006. Sony (television and components) employs 2,200 people locally for second place.

What does the "33" on all bottles of Rolling Rock beer represent?

The makers of the beer have no official explanation, although some theories exist. One is that 1933 was the end of prohibition in the U.S.

How many Fortune 500 companies were headquartered in Pittsburgh in 1966?

20.

How many Fortune 500 companies are headquartered in the Pittsburgh area today?

Six. They are: U.S. Steel, PPG, PNC, H.J. Heinz, Mellon, and WESCO.

In the six-county Pittsburgh region, how many jobs are there?

In mid-year 2005, there were about 1,191,000 workers on employer payrolls.

In tonnage, what is the most heavily-transported commodity on area rivers?

It's coal. In 2002, of the 52 million tons of goods and materials shipped on area rivers, 40.1 million tons were coal. A combination of sand, gravel, rock, and stone made up another 4.2 million tons.

Based on sales, what's the biggest area supply company headed by a woman?

It's 84 Lumber, whose head person is Maggie Hardy Magerko. The company with sales of $3.64 billion in 2004 was started by Maggie's father, Joe Hardy.

How many cases of Iron City beer products are produced each year?

About 5,852,250 cases.

How much did advertisers spend on Pittsburgh-area radio stations in 2004?

About $112 million. In 1999, sales were about $100 million.

How much money did advertisers spend on Pittsburgh-area television stations in 2004?

About $225 million. That's about $8 million less than five years ago.

The Pittsburgh Film Office opened in 1990. Since then, how much money has film production pumped into the Pittsburgh area?

Film production has brought about $266 million into the local economy.

In terms of assets, what are the Pittsburgh-area's five largest foundations (figures are from 2004)?

Richard King Mellon Foundation ($1.6 billion); Howard Heinz Endowment ($862 million); The Pittsburgh Foundation ($537 million); McCune Foundation ($520 million); Vira I. Heinz Endowment ($445 million.)

What is the dollar value of Pittsburgh-area exports to the rest of the world?

$3.940 billion. The figures are from 1999, the last year the federal government collected figures. One third of the total consists of chemical products.

What area residential real estate sales people sold the most residential units and had the highest dollar volume in residential sales in 2004?

The most residential units were sold by Alyce Jean Duffus (Choice Homes Duffus/Epps). She sold 298 units. Linda Honeywill (Prudential Realty) had the highest dollar value: $42 million in residential sales.

How much money did the United Way of Allegheny County raise in its 2005 campaign? What charities received allocations?

The campaign raised $30,094,431 in 2005. The five charities getting the largest allocations (2005 figures): Catholic Charities, Pittsburgh Diocese ($1,033,582); American Red Cross ($980,071); Salvation Army ($926,213); Boys and Girls Clubs of Western PA/Campfire ($888,979); YMCA of Greater Pittsburgh ($789,809).

Of the $3.940 billion in Pittsburgh area exports, four countries receive over 50 percent of the total. What are those four countries?

Canada imports 35.8 percent of Pittsburgh area products; Mexico, 10 percent; Germany, 4.6 percent; and the United Kingdom, 4.4 percent.

What product is the Pittsburgh area's biggest export commodity?

Chemicals. Chemicals represent 30.6 percent of everything exported from the Pittsburgh area. That is $1.102 billion worth of products. Industrial machinery and computers (17.1 percent of the total, worth $617 million) come in second. Third, are primary metals, mostly steel (13.1 percent of the total, worth $471 million). Total exports are $3.940 billion.

Percentage-wise, what occupation does the state say will have the biggest gain between now and 2010 in the Pittsburgh area?

For the most part, no surprise here. The percentage gains are mainly in the computer field. Between now and 2010, there will be a 54.7 percent gain among computer support specialists, a 42.3 percent gain among computer software engineers and computer network administrators, and a 41.7 percent gain among network systems and data communications analysts. The surprise? A 41.9 percent gain among locomotive engineers.

What occupation does the state say will have the greatest number of job openings between now and 2010 in the Pittsburgh area?

Between now and 2010 the largest numbers of jobs will be retail sales cashiers (1,873 jobs) and retail salespersons (1,805 jobs). There will be openings for an additional 1,158 food preparation and serving workers. In third place? The 513 secondary school teachers needed in special and vocational education.

In the Pittsburgh area, what is the average annual wage for the following occupations: Accountants and auditors, architects, bill collectors, chefs and head cooks, chemists, computer programmers, drywall and ceiling tile installers, electrical engineers, janitors and cleaners, medical and clinical lab technicians, pharmacists, paralegals, real estate brokers, roofers, security guards, surgeons, telemarketers, truck drivers (heavy and tractor trailer), welders?

Accountants and auditors ($50,570); architects ($55,850); bill collectors ($25,400); chefs and head cooks ($35,090); chemists ($55,010); computer programmers ($54,620); drywall and ceiling tile installers ($32,320); electrical engineers ($68,120); janitors and cleaners ($20,540); medical and clinical lab technicians ($32,000); paralegals ($33,120); pharmacists ($71,090); real estate brokers ($60,390); roofers ($31,780); security guards ($17,670); surgeons ($191,240); telemarketers ($23,910); truck drivers (heavy and tractor trailer) ($36,380); welders ($31,750).

What was the first labor union to organize in Pittsburgh?

The Typographical Union Local 7. It was formed in 1836 and is still going strong.

Based on sales, what are the area's largest privately-owned companies?

Giant Eagle ($4.7 billion in revenue); 84 Lumber ($2.2 billion); Dick Corp ($93.5 million); Koppers ($843 million); Copperweld ($767 million).

Who are the area's biggest employers of full-time employees?

UPMC Health System (26,700 employees); U.S. Government (19,400); Commonwealth of PA (13,300); West Penn Allegheny Health System (10,700); University of Pittsburgh (10,100).

What are the area's largest public companies ranked by sales?

Alcoa ($21.5 billion); U.S. Steel ($9.5); PPG Industries ($8.7); H.J. Heinz ($8.4); Nova Chemicals ($3.9).

What three credit unions in the Pittsburgh area have the most assets?

Clearview Federal Credit Union (formerly USAirways FCU) ($618 million); Butler Armco Employees Credit Union ($196 million); MonValley Community FCU ($116 million).

What was the average annual wage earning for workers in the Pittsburgh area in 2005?

Allegheny County ($35,835); Beaver County ($31,244); Butler County ($31,369); Fayette County ($29,710); Washington County ($33,341); Westmoreland County ($31,841).

True or False: Duquesne Club members may examine contents of briefcases or other business documents only in private rooms or private suites.

True. Do not open your briefcase in a non-private dining room, lounge or corridor. The rules for cell phones are just as strict. At least the Club's post-meal macaroons are free.

Years ago, the Duquesne Club catered to the city's white business elite. What club did Pittsburgh's African American elite join?

The Loendi Club. The club was founded on August 13, 1897 in the city's Hill District. It supposedly was named after a river in Africa.

How many people work in the city of Pittsburgh?

About 325,000. Starting in 2005, each worker pays a $52 occupation tax to the city. From 1965 until 2005, the tax was $10. The tax is formally known, now, as the Emergency and Municipal Services Tax.

What is the highest-assessed piece of real estate in Allegheny County?

For taxable property, it is the One Mellon Center, which has an estimated value of $285.5 million.

In 1993, the Pittsburgh area had 13 venture capital firms with $620 million to invest. How many venture capital firms are in the Pittsburgh area now and how much money do they have under management?

In early 2005, the Pittsburgh Business Times *lists 25 venture capital firms with about $9.5 billion to invest.*

A t one time, what did it mean to be "Westinghoused"?

It meant to be electrocuted. In the early 1900s, there was a debate over whether direct current (DC) or alternating current (AC) was the safer way to deliver electricity. Thomas Edison favored DC, Pittsburgher George Westinghouse favored AC. Edison came up with the term to describe the fate of someone who had been executed by the electric chair. Needless to say, the Pittsburgher won.

H ow many square feet of retail space are in downtown Pittsburgh's central business district?

A little over 2 million square feet.

I n the Pittsburgh region, what were the total retail sales in 2002?

About $25.138 billion. In 1997, total retail sales were about $21.5 billion.

A t the retail level, do Pittsburgh area people spend more money on automobiles or on food and beverages?

In 2002, motor vehicles and parts dealers had sales of about $6.39 billion. The figure for food and beverages was $4.06 billion. Retail sales in grocery stores was $3.45 billion.

J . Vincent McBride is by no stretch of the imagination a household name although he created a household product used in millions of homes throughout the world. What did he create: dry wall, liquid drain cleaner or Romex?

McBride created Romex, which is plastic insulated housing wire. He is from Washington, PA and a graduate of Carnegie Tech (1932). He died in 1997.

W hat tall order did TRACO, a local window manufacturer, successfully fulfill in 1992?

*TRACO replaced 6,742 windows in the Empire State Build-
ing.*

I n 1997, LTV Steel closed its Hazelwood facilities and laid off 750
workers. Along with the 750 lost jobs, the Pittsburgh-area environ-
ment lost 1,095 tons of sulfur dioxide, 1,806 tons of nitrogen oxide
and 324 tons of airborne particles. What product caused the pollution?

Coke.

W hat company on the North Side has a red neon, 30-foot bottle
spelling out its name and gurgling out its product while simultaneously flashing the time and weather?

*The H. J. Heinz Company. A good view is from the Veterans
Bridge (I-579).*

W hen did Braddock's Edgar Thomson Works (now part of U.S.
Steel) first produce steel?

*In 1875. The first output was turned into 2,000 steel rails for
the Pennsylvania Railroad. The plant is still in operation. At its
peak during World War II, the plant had 5,000 employees. Now
it has fewer than 1,000.*

T he Joy Cone Company in Hermitage, Pennsylvania is the largest ice
cream cone company in the world. How many cones does it bake
each year to achieve that title?

1.5 billion. The company started in 1918.

What Pittsburgh-area facility in the 1950s designed nuclear reactors for the first atomic submarine (USS *Nautilus*), aircraft carrier (USS *Enterprise*) and commercial power plant (Shippingport) to supply electricity?

The Bettis Atomic Power Laboratory in West Mifflin. The reactors were designed when Westinghouse Electric owned Bettis. Now the plant is owned by Bechtel Bettis, Inc. The location has a history of supplying energy. In 1795, Joseph Large Jr. distilled Monongahela Pure Rye whiskey there.

Every employee of the S-shaped Alcoa Corporation Center on the banks of the Allegheny River has a view of what?

Downtown and the river. No employee sits more than 45 feet from an exterior window.

What Pittsburgher, in addition to Andrew W. Mellon, served as the U.S. secretary of the treasury?

Paul O'Neill left as chairman and CEO of Alcoa to serve under President George W. Bush from January 2001 to December 2002. Mellon served between 1921 and 1930 under three presidents.

Prime Outlets at Grove City in Mercer County has over 140 shops. How many shoppers go there a year searching for a good deal?

About 4.7 million people drop in at the outlets, which opened in August 1994. The spot has over 535,000 square feet of shops.

Pennsylvania Lubricating Company is famous for what?

The company, in the Strip District, was the first grease manufacturing plant in the U.S. It started business in 1885, eventually becoming part of Exxon. During World War II, it supplied five million pounds of "Eisenhower grease."

A World War II Bantam Jeep. Courtesy of Leeland V. Bortmas.

Butler County's American Bantam Car Company designed, developed and built a vehicle recognized around the world. What is it?

Bantam designed the jeep, short for General Purpose Vehicle. In 1940, the U.S. government hosted a design competition for a vehicle with four-wheel drive, 40-horsepower and weighing a maximum of 1,300 pounds. American Bantam won and then built about 2,675 jeeps before Pearl Harbor. Unfortunately, the company never got a contract to build more because it couldn't meet the quantity needed for the war. Ford and Willys-Overland eventually built 600,000 jeeps. American Bantam closed in 1956.

This is not a silly question. Rob Roy McGregor, from Verona, and Earl Warrick, a Pittsburgher, filed a patent in 1943 for a well-known product. What is the product?

Silly Putty. At the time they were working for Corning Glass.

What local company had the original patent for Formica?

Westinghouse Electric. While working for Westinghouse, Daniel O'Connor, Jr. and Herbert Faber came up with the product in 1913. Westinghouse was not interested in the product so O'Connor and Faber left to start Formica Corporation.

What company was the first to use a ring-pull can for its product?

Iron City Brewing.

What local steel company played a role/roll (both) in the building of the Guggenheim Museum in Bilbao, Spain?

Allegheny Ludlum. A company from Colorado sent thick rolls of titanium to Allegheny Ludlum to "hot roll" (make thinner). After reducing the titanium's thickness, Allegheny Ludlum sent the metal on its way to becoming the outer skin of the museum. This skin is less than a millimeter thick, incidentally.

At one time, it was the world's largest natural gas storage facility. Now, it is merely the largest one in Pennsylvania. Where is it?

Dominion Peoples has a natural gas storage field near Murrysville – the biggest in the state. It is approximately 11 by 5 miles in size. The gas is stored in two layers, between 700 and 7,800 feet deep, and a mind-blowing 120 billion cubic feet of gas can be stored there. The gas comes from as far away as the Gulf of Mexico. The facility uses strata of sandstone and limestone.

Pittsburgh was the first big U.S. city to have natural gas piped into it. When?

In January 1883. The gas came from Murrysville, 25 miles from Pittsburgh. The gas was used mainly to manufacture glass and the gas line was at 16th Street in the Strip District.

How big are the Mellon logos and letters on top of One Mellon Bank Center?

The circular logo is 23 feet in diameter and the letters are 14 feet high. The signs are on the building's northern and southern sides.

Left: *Miners pushing an "empty" near Pittsburgh, PA. H. C. White Co., Chicago, 1907. Library of Congress, LC-USZ62-96861.* Right: *Boring for a blast. H. C. White Co., Chicago, 1907. Library of Congress, LC-USZ62-96863.*

In 1914, what Pittsburgh company joined with Thomas Edison to devise a product to save the lives of coal miners?

It was Mine Safety Appliances (MSA). MSA and Edison made a flameless electric miner's cap that safely provided light underground. Open-flamed cap lamps, in use before the MSA/Edison helmet and the source of ignition, would combine with methane gas, oxygen and coal dust to cause underground explosions.

What was USAirways called when it started business in 1937?

It started as All-American Aviation, then Allegheny Airlines (or Agony Airlines to critics), USAir and finally, USAirways. All-American Aviation handled only mail. Paying passengers first boarded in 1949.

Jenny Lee Bakery in McKees Rocks started business in 1875 as the Michael Baker Bakery. Next, the company's name became Seven Baker Brothers Bakery and, finally, in 1938, Jenny Lee Bakery. What is the origin of the Jenny Lee name?

Members of the Baker family were on their way to a meeting to apply for a loan and they needed a new company name. A song, Sweet Jenny Lee From Sunny Tennessee, came on the radio and that was music to the Bakers' ears.

What hotel and office building were demolished to make way for One Mellon Center at Fifth Avenue and Ross Street downtown?

The Carlton House Hotel and the Plaza Building.

What plant in Lawrence County is the oldest continuously operated cement-making operation in the United States?

The Wampum Cement and Lime Co., Limited started business in 1874. The company is now known as CEMEX.

What are the last four digits in Heinz USA's phone number?

5757, what else?

At the western edge of The Waterfront at the old USX Steel Plant in Homestead is a line of very large stacks, each 110 feet high. How many stacks are there and what was their original use?

There are 12 stacks built in 1944. They were used to vent steam that formed whenever steel ingots were soaked and heated in pits prior to being rolled into slabs.

BEYOND THE 'BURGH

Chapel of the Holy Spirit at the Vatican. Courtesy Astorino.

The Chapel of the Holy Spirit, inside Vatican City, was designed by a Pittsburgh architect. Who?

> *Lou Astorino designed the chapel, which was dedicated in 1996. The chapel is used for daily mass. Cardinals will use the chapel whenever they gather at a conclave to elect a new pope. Astorino and his associates have also designed the Trimont condos on Mount Washington as well as PNC Firstside Center and the new Pittsburgh Municipal Courts building on First Avenue.*

How many Academy Awards in all categories were won by films made in the Pittsburgh area?

> *Ten.* The Deer Hunter *and* The Silence of the Lambs *each won five. There were 31 nominations for all movies filmed here.*

In what city would you find Don Knotts Boulevard?

In Morgantown, WV, Knotts's hometown. He played deputy Barney Fife on the old Andy Griffith Show. *Knotts died in February, 2006.*

Sarah B. Cochran, the widow of a Fayette County coke and coal businessman, built a mansion in 1913 at a cost of $2 million. The place has 35 rooms, 27 fireplaces, 13 baths with 8,720 square feet on each floor. It is named after the trees Ms. Cochran brought in from Berlin and planted throughout the grounds. What is the mansion's name?

Linden Hall. The place has Tiffany Studio's stained glass windows and an Aeolian pipe organ, one of only three in the world. Linden Hall is in Dawson Borough, Fayette County.

It is hard not to notice a 40-plus-foot high figure sculpture with 15 bronze figures that are each about nine feet high. This one-ton sculpture is possibly the largest figure sculpture in Western Pennsylvania. Its title is *Ascent of Humanity*. Where is it?

It is on a wall of California University's World Culture Building in Washington County.

For what was the oil first discovered at Oil City used?

As an illuminant in lamps. Originally, oil people thought oil would begin to compete with coal as a source of lighting.

How long is Altoona's horseshoe curve and what is it?

The semi-circle curve is about 1,400 feet across and its arc is nearly one mile long. It opened in 1854 and was built using picks, shovels and horses. The curve was built by the Pennsylvania Railroad.

How did Uniontown get its name?

Around 1776, Uniontown started out as Beeson's-town but was renamed as an allusion to the federal union.

When and where did America's deadliest flash flood occur?

The day was May 31, 1889. A 72 foot high, 930-foot dam broke about 24 miles from Johnstown, PA. At one point, the water hit a height of 76 feet. The death toll was 2,209. The dam, which was built in 1852, was in a state of disrepair even though some repairs had been made to it.

What Western Pennsylvania county calls itself the "Tool and Die Capital of the World"?

Crawford County. The county has more than 300 tool and die shops.

What Pittsburgh area municipality has the longest one-word name? (That is, one whose name is not preceded, or followed by an adjective like North, New, South, etc.)

Connoquenessing in Butler County. There are a borough and a township with the same name.

What local popular recreation site has a name that is American Indian in origin and means "white frothy water?"

The site is Ohiopyle. At one time Delaware, Shawnee and Iroquois hunted in the area. The origin of the word is "Ohiopehhle," which means "white frothy water" in certain Native American languages. They, of course, were referring to the large falls on the Youghiogheny River.

What do the town of Saxonburg and the Brooklyn Bridge have in common?

John Roebling, who emigrated to Saxonburg, devised a plan for the town and also designed the Brooklyn Bridge. Roebling invented wire "rope" cable, making suspension bridge design possible.

The towns of Harmony in Butler County and Old Economy in Beaver County have something in common. What is it?

Each was organized in the early 19th century by followers of George Rapp, a charismatic German religious leader. The members of the faith were called Harmonists.

When did a fire destroy the West View Dance Land?

On October 3, 1973. The West View Amusement Park closed four years later. The West View Shopping Center now occupies the land of the old park.

What Beaver County bridge's name is decided annually by the outcome of a high school football game?

The winner of the game between Rochester and Monaca high schools determines whether it is the Monaca/Rochester Bridge or vice versa.

What is Pennsylvania's largest state park?

It is Ohiopyle State Park, in Fayette County, which has 18,719 acres. For a comparison, Point State Park in Pittsburgh has 36 acres. The total size of Pymatuning State Park is 21,122 acres but more than half of that is Pymatuning Lake.

In what year did the town of Donora have a smog inversion which led to the death of 25 people?

October, 1948. Over 6,000 people were taken ill. Steel mill pollution combined with smog caused the problem.

Where and when was the first crematorium built in the United States?

In Washington, PA in 1876.

Where do high school seniors drive tractors to school on the day of the prom?

At Riverside High School in North Sewickley Township, Beaver County.

Where is the only place in the world with an actual Mister Rogers' Neighborhood?

It is in Idlewild Park in Ligonier, Westmoreland County.

Where is the world's first atomic-powered electric plant located?

In Shippingport, Beaver County. Duquesne Light started to ship atomic-powered electricity to Pittsburgh on December 18, 1957.

What was so unusual about the 1997 graduating class at Beaver County's Riverside High School?

Three of its graduates entered West Point. Not only that, all three were women.

Where is the largest American Indian burial mound in Pennsylvania?

It is in McKees Rocks. The mound is 16 1/2 feet tall and 85 feet in diameter. The Indians were known as the Adena people. Scientists from the Carnegie Museum of Natural History excavated the mound in 1896; the mound may date back to 250 B.C.

The 135-mile Youghiogheny River forms near the western edge of Maryland, flows north and enters the Monongahela River at McKeesport. What does Youghiogheny mean?

The Youghiogheny is the only river in Western Maryland that does not flow south into the Potomac River. As a result, the river's name comes from the Algonquian Indian word that means "contrary stream."

Moraine State Park in Butler County is over 15,000 acres. How big is Lake Arthur, which is in the park?

The actual lake is 3,225 acres.

Zippo cigarette lighters have been manufactured in Bradford, Pennsylvania since 1932. How many have been made since then?

Over 250 million.

What is the largest natural lake located entirely in Pennsylvania?

The 928-acre Conneaut Lake.

How big is Pymatuning Lake in Crawford County?

This favorite recreational spot for many Pennsylvanians has a total acreage of 21,122, with the lake occupying 13,716 acres.

By no means a handyman's special, Haley House is the oldest house in nearby Beaver County. Courtesy of the Beaver County Historical Research Landmarks Foundation from A Guide to Historic Landmarks in Beaver County, Pennsylvania, *2002.*

What is the oldest residential structure in Beaver County?

A weather-boarded log house at 191 Oakville Road in Chippewa Township built by John Haley in 1792.

On November 12, 1955, Albert Miller, owner of a piece of property in Avella, Pennsylvania, came across a groundhog hole on the site. He enlarged the hole and found a flint knife in it. What, eventually, did the groundhog hole become known as?

The Meadowcroft Rock Shelter, a campsite, has the oldest evidence of Native American life in North America dating to about 16,000 years ago. Miller, an amateur archaeologist, feared looters and kept quiet about the site until 1973 when he found a professional to examine his findings. The site contains food remains, animal bones, tools and basketing.

When it comes to polo, the biggest "buzz" surrounds the Breakers in Palm Beach, Florida. The Pittsburgh area, however, has the oldest, continuous polo club in the U.S. Where is it?

It's the Darlington Polo Club in Darlington, PA (Beaver County).

The author beside the oldest tree in Allegheny County. Courtesy of Jack Moore.

Dane Topich was born, raised and still lives on Pittsburgh's South Side. He worked at KDKA-TV and Radio for over 17 years as editorial director and public affairs manager; before that, he worked on numerous political campaigns. A graduate of the University of Pittsburgh with a degree in political science, he can still be seen hanging out on Carson Street.

I N D E X

Page numbers in italics refer to photographs;
a "t" after a page number refers to a table.

Here's your chance to participate in the next version of *Ultimate Pittsburgh Trivia*.

If you have a trivia question and an answer that can be verified, mail it to:

Dane Topich c/o Towers Maguire Publishing at the address below.

YOU MUST INCLUDE YOUR SOURCE FOR THE QUESTION/ ANSWER SO THAT IT CAN BE VERIFIED. Include your full name and contact information. The author will only notify you if your question and answer are used.
